Devotions with Presidents

By Timothy D. Holder

Author Website: www.tdhcommunications.com

Acknowledgements

There are many people who contributed in one way or another to this book, and to them I am extremely grateful.

Jeff Bohanan spent a year telling me that this kind of book was what I needed to write, so I wrote *Presidential Stories*, and he turned out to be right. *Devotions with Presidents* is just more of the same. It's funny how listening to really smart people helps me out in life.

Ashley Schwartz is an excellent editor, and I am so pleased she agreed to work with me. She caught grammar and editing issues, and she was really great about explaining why things were wrong, so I learned more about the mechanics of writing (and it guaranteed I wouldn't argue with her). Ashley also helped with phrasing and readability, and she even offered great ideas about themes and Scripture verses.

Dan Lyle contributed his time and talent in creating fantastic cover art. I greatly appreciated his ability, his generosity, and his positive spirit. And I would like to add a "thank you" here to Kristen Golliher for providing the picture of me. I believe she said at the time that it would be good enough for a book cover. It looks like she was right.

Kristin Haney was kind enough to contribute a bonus devotion to these pages. Her work is completely different from the rest of the book, which makes it great as an extra feature. Kristin gives the reader something unique. I am so pleased that she was willing to share her time and talent. And I appreciated her conscientious and diligent approach to the project.

Steve Ellis of Light House Studio has done a great job over the years with my website. It's not his fault that I am slow to update the content—Steve always holds up his end of the bargain. He does great work.

When I had a question about the cover art, feedback was helpfully, cheerfully, and promptly provided by Amanda Bohanan, Kay Brown, Lee Couture, Tina Maddox, Kim Nichols, and Amy

Williams. They were all encouraging and funny—two traits that I highly value.

Alyssa Derrington, Travis Gordon, John Green IV, Joseph North, Jeff Stewardson, Sheri Stewardson, Donny Wadley, and Greg Williams all helped by giving me useful material for content. It was usually unintentional on their part, which actually made it better. They are just that wise. (And for the record, I didn't use anything without their consent.)

List of Devotions by Day, President, and Scripture Passage

1.   Abraham Lincoln, Hebrews 6:1
2.   John Kennedy, Richard Nixon, Joshua 1:9
3.   Barack Obama, Matthew 22:37
4.   George Washington, Matthew 5:16
5.   Theodore Roosevelt, William Taft, Matthew 6:12
6.   George W. Bush, 2 Timothy 1:7
7.   Abraham Lincoln, Luke 14:8
8.   Bill Clinton, Psalm 51:2-3
9.   Abraham Lincoln, Matthew 7:12
10.   Ronald Reagan, Galatians 5:22-23
11.   Abraham Lincoln, Colossians 3:13
12.   George HW Bush, Proverbs 11:13
13.   William McKinley, Genesis 2:24
14.   Jimmy Carter, 1 Corinthians 10:31
15.   Millard Fillmore, Psalm 73:1
16.   Thomas Jefferson, Psalm 26:4
17.   Martin Van Buren, 1 Corinthians 13:12
18.   Richard Nixon, Exodus 32:4
19.   Barack Obama, Matthew 6:14
20.   John Tyler, Matthew 6:5A
21.   Andrew Johnson, Ezekiel 13:9A
22.   Theodore Roosevelt, 1Thessalonians 4:13
23.   Franklin Roosevelt, Deuteronomy 31:6
24.   George Washington, Hebrews 13:8
25.   Jimmy Carter, Matthew 5:16
26.   Benjamin Harrison, Ephesians 6:18
27.   Theodore Roosevelt, Philippians 2:14
28.   Thomas Jefferson, James Madison, Luke 16:8A
29.   Grover Cleveland, Galatians 3:13-14
30.   Abraham Lincoln, Genesis 3:12-13
31.   Richard Nixon, 1 Corinthians 15:33
32.   Ulysses Grant, Matthew 25:24-27
33.   Franklin Roosevelt, Proverbs 22:29
34.   Andrew Jackson, 2 Timothy 1:7

35.   Abraham Lincoln, Psalm 27:1
36.   William McKinley, 1 Peter 4:10
37.   George W. Bush, Philippians 1:9
38.   John Tyler, Colossians 3:12
39.   Richard Nixon, Isaiah 40:31
40.   William Harrison, Genesis 12:1
41.   Donald Trump, 2 Timothy 3:16-17
42.   John Quincy Adams, 1 Thessalonians 5:22
43.   Ulysses Grant, Romans 12:18
44.   Andrew Johnson, Proverbs 18:2
45.   Harry Truman, Psalm 17:6
46.   William McKinley, 1 Peter 2:13A
47.   Abraham Lincoln, 1 Peter 5:6-7
48.   Abraham Lincoln, Matthew 17:21
49.   Dwight Eisenhower, Acts 13:1-2
50.   John Adams, Ephesians 3:20-21
51.   Zachary Taylor, Proverbs 25:11
52.   William Taft, Acts 9:5-6
53.   George Washington, Acts 13:39-40
54.   Andrew Jackson, Psalm 29:3
55.   Calvin Coolidge, Romans 13:8
56.   Ronald Reagan, Jeremiah 29:11
57.   Andrew Jackson, 1 Peter 1:15-16
58.   George HW Bush, Colossians 3:14
59.   James Polk, James 1:5
60.   Zachary Taylor, Colossians 3:15
61.   Theodore Roosevelt, 2 Timothy 2:15
62.   James Monroe, Proverbs 11:2
63.   Abraham Lincoln, Philippians 4:7
64.   James Buchanan, 1 Thessalonians 5:11
65.   Franklin Pierce, Colossians 1:11
66.   Ulysses Grant, Proverbs 27:17
67.   Andrew Johnson, 1 Corinthians 6:14
68.   Garfield, Kennedy, GW Bush, Ruth 1:16
69.   George Washington, Proverbs 10:9
70.   George Washington, Woodrow Wilson, Phil. 3:17

71. George Washington, Galatians 6:9
72. Abraham Lincoln, Proverbs 16:18
73. James Garfield, Galatians 6:5
74. Franklin Roosevelt, Isaiah 49:15-16
75. Donald Trump, Matthew 15:7-9
76. James Garfield, 1 Peter, 4:10
77. Harry Truman, Ecclesiastes 4:12.
78. John Adams, James 4:17
79. Richard Nixon, Romans 3:23.
80. John Adams, 1 Samuel 16:23.
81. Thomas Jefferson, Exodus 14:14.
82. John Quincy Adams, John 14:6.
83. Harry Truman, 1 Peter 4:8.
84. Chester Arthur, Ephesians 3:12.
85. Barack Obama, James 1:19.
86. Thomas Jefferson, 1 Peter 2:16.
87. James Polk, Psalm 101:2A.
88. Lyndon Johnson, Psalm 119:9.
89. James Buchanan, Psalm 86:5.
90. William Howard Taft, 1 Corinthians 6:19-20.
91. Warren Harding, Judges 6:15.
92. Andrew Johnson, Philippians 3:12.
93. Warren Harding, Psalm 37:4
94. Benjamin Harrison, Matthew 26:41
95. Ronald Reagan, Hebrews 12:14
96. Lyndon Johnson, James 1:27
97. James Madison, Proverbs 19:20
98. Richard Nixon, Romans 14:12
99. George Washington, Matthew 25:23
100. Andrew Jackson, Psalm 4:4
101. John Kennedy, Exodus 20:17
102. George Washington, Romans 14:13
103. Jimmy Carter, Romans 16:12
104. Bill Clinton, John 3:16
105. Dwight Eisenhower, Romans 8:28
106. Gerald Ford, Proverbs 24:10

107. Theodore Roosevelt, 1 Samuel 16:7
108. Millard Fillmore, Isaiah 2:12
109. James Madison, Leviticus 19:34
110. Abraham Lincoln, 1 Samuel 13:14A
111. George Washington, Psalm 20:7
112. Chester Arthur, Luke 9:25
113. Dwight Eisenhower, Matthew 21:12
114. Dwight Eisenhower, Richard Nixon, Luke 23:34A
115. Grover Cleveland, 1 Corinthians 7:35
116. Theodore Roosevelt, John 11:43-44
117. Harry Truman, Mark 16:15
118. George Washington, James Madison, John 1:45-46
119. Ronald Reagan, Psalm 35:18
120. Rutherford Hayes, Proverbs 26:13
121. Richard Nixon, Titus 2:1
122. Theodore Roosevelt, Hebrews 12:11
123. Andrew Johnson, Colossians 4:6
124. Abraham Lincoln, Philippians 4:5
125. Benjamin Harrison, Colossians 4:2
126. Woodrow Wilson, Matthew 10:16
127. James Madison, Acts 16:6
128. Herbert Hoover, Romans 8:37
129. John Adams, Proverbs 27:4
130. John Adams, Ephesians 5:21
131. Benjamin Harrison, Romans 5:3-4
132. Ulysses Grant, Joshua 10:25A
133. Herbert Hoover, Psalm 30:5
134. Grover Cleveland, 2 Corinthians 7:1
135. James Polk, 1 Corinthians 10:31
136. Richard Nixon, Matthew 5:44
137. Millard Fillmore, James 4:14B
138. Rutherford Hayes, Luke 7:34
139. Rutherford B. Hayes, Romans 10:13-15
140. Chester Arthur, Ephesians 4:29
141. John Kennedy, Colossians 3:5-6
142. Abraham Lincoln, Ephesians 6:14

143.   Franklin Pierce, Psalm 32:8
144.   Thomas Jefferson, Romans 10:1
145.   James Buchanan, 1 Corinthians 16:14
146.   Abraham Lincoln, Psalm 34:14
147.   William Howard Taft, Luke 6:36
148.   James Monroe, John 15:13
149.   Franklin Pierce, Ephesians 4:31
150.   George Washington, Thomas Jefferson, Ephesians 4:32

Devotions by President

1.   George Washington: Day 4, 24, 53, 69, 70, 71, 99, 102, 111, 118, and 150
2.   John Adams: Days 50, 78, 80, 129 and 130
3.   Thomas Jefferson: Days 16, 28, 81, 86, 144, and 150
4.   James Madison: Days 28, 97, 109, 118, and 127
5.   James Monroe: Days 62 and 148
6.   John Quincy Adams: Days 42 and 82
7.   Andrew Jackson: Days 34, 54, 57, and 100
8.   Martin Van Buren: Day 17
9.   William Henry Harrison: Day 40
10.   John Tyler: Days 20 and 38
11.   James Polk: Days 59, 87, and 135
12.   Zachary Taylor: Days 51 and 60
13.   Milliard Fillmore: Days 15, 108, and 137
14.   Franklin Pierce: Days 143 and 149
15.   James Buchanan: Days 64, 89, and 145
16.   Abraham Lincoln: Days 1, 7, 9, 11, 30, 35, 47, 48, 63, 72, 110, 124, 142, and 146
17.   Andrew Johnson: Days 21, 44, 67, 92, and 123
18.   Ulysses Grant: Days 32, 43, 66, and 132
19.   Rutherford B. Hayes: Days 120, 138, and 139
20.   James Garfield: Days 68, 73, and 76
21.   Chester Arthur: Days 84, 112, and 140
22.   Grover Cleveland: Days 29, 115, and 134
23.   Benjamin Harrison: Days 26, 94, 125, and 131

24.   Grover Cleveland: Days 29, 115, and 134
25.   William McKinley: Days 13, 36, and 46
26.   Theodore Roosevelt: Days 5, 22, 27, 61, 107, 116, and 122
27.   William Howard Taft: Days 5, 52, 90, and 147
28.   Woodrow Wilson: Days 70 and 126
29.   Warren Harding: Days 91 and 93
30.   Calvin Coolidge: Day 55
31.   Herbert Hoover: Days 128 and 133
32.   Franklin Roosevelt: Days 23, 33, and 74
33.   Harry Truman: Days 45, 77, 83, and 117
34.   Dwight Eisenhower: Days 49, 105, 113, and 114
35.   John Kennedy: Days 2, 68, 101, and 141
36.   Lyndon Johnson: Days 88 and 96
37.   Richard Nixon: Days 2, 18, 31, 39, 79, 98, 114, 121, and 136
38.   Gerald Ford: Day 106
39.   Jimmy Carter: Days 14, 25, and 103
40.   Ronald Reagan: Days 10, 56, 95, and 119
41.   George HW Bush: Days 12 and 58
42.   Bill Clinton: Days 8 and 104
43.   George W. Bush: Days 6, 37, and 68
44.   Barack Obama: Days 3, 19, and 85
45.   Donald Trump: Days 41 and 75

Day 1

Abraham Lincoln

Hebrews 6:1 "Therefore, let us leave the elementary teaching about Christ and go on to maturity, not laying again a foundation of repentance from dead works, faith in God."

On January 1, 1863, Abraham Lincoln's Emancipation Proclamation went into effect. Some people (and by "some people" I actually mean "most people") believe the Emancipation Proclamation ended slavery.

It didn't.

The document declared that slaves who were in the Rebel states which were still in rebellion would be considered legally free in the eyes of the Union. Thus, slavery in the northern border states (Kentucky, Maryland, etc.) was still legal, and it was legal in the Confederate state that the Union had already retaken (Tennessee).

It was the 13th Amendment, which went into effect in 1865 several months after the Civil War was over, that ended slavery. That's right: Ironically, there were some slaves in the North after slavery in the South had been ended.

The point here is not to stir up arguments or regional pride. The point is that some changes can be hard and gradual. In fact, even before the American Revolution ended in the 1780s, some people in America had already begun chipping away at the institution of slavery.

Change can be hard. Sometimes, we have to play the long game, and we need that reminder in a society geared towards instant gratification. As we try to change and grow spiritually, it might not come easily. We might slow down, stop, or fall back. But let us pray that we will keep chipping away at our sinful nature and bad habits. Let's keep praying and pushing in the right direction.

Day 2

John Kennedy and Richard Nixon

Joshua 1:9 "Haven't I commanded you: be strong and courageous? Do not be afraid or discouraged for the Lord your God is with you wherever you go."

On January 2, 1960, John Kennedy announced his candidacy for the presidency. Was he too young? Would Nixon be too hard to beat? Was this the right time?

When a lot of people think about Kennedy, they see a young (for the presidency), good looking, charismatic guy. How could that crook, Richard Nixon, have been any kind of threat to candidate Kennedy?

Actually, Nixon looked pretty formidable back then. Both men were in their 40s when they ran against each other in 1960. Nixon, like Kennedy, had served in both the House and the Senate, and they were also World War Two veterans, seeing time in the Pacific Theater. And Nixon had something on his resume that Kennedy didn't: Nixon had served two terms as the VP for the quite popular Dwight Eisenhower. Nixon was a really strong candidate on paper, so it would not have been shocking if Kennedy had decided to wait and challenge a lesser opponent later.

As we know, Kennedy decided to compete anyway, and he won. "You miss 100% of the shots you don't take," said Wayne Gretzky.

Okay, so that's not technically true, but you still get the idea.

Sometimes we choose not to do the big thing we are called to do; sometimes we hesitate, and the opportunity is lost. We need to pray for faith enough to be strong and courageous and take that bold step required of us today.

Day 3

Barack Obama

Matthew 22:37 "He said to him, 'Love the Lord your God with all your heart, with all your soul, and with all your mind.'"

On January 3, 2008, voting took place in Iowa to begin the process of picking candidates for the presidency. For the Democrats, Barack Obama won his first victory on his way to shocking the Clinton Machine* and winning the Democratic nomination (and eventually the presidency).

For Republicans, Mike Huckabee was the winner. But this party eventually settled on John McCain in 2008. As Huckabee would later say after his daughter became a press secretary for President Trump, "I knew there would be a Huckabee in the White House. I just didn't know which one."

Both Obama and Huckabee had the same result in Iowa, but it ultimately took them on a different journey. What is interesting about this is some of us spend a lot of time and energy reading into situations and developments, and trying to assign some kind of meaning to them.

"God didn't let me have this thing I wanted, so I bet there is something better right around the corner."

"God didn't let me have this thing I wanted. I must need to learn some kind of lesson. Once I learn it, God will make things better."

"It was successful at X, so surely God now wants X + Y."

God is not always so subtle. He is pretty straightforward in His Word regarding what He wants us to do: Love Him completely. The execution is tough, but the command pretty clear. Instead of trying to divine the future based on our perceptions of the present, let's today focus on the obvious thing God told us: Let's love Him.

*This is just an expression. Clinton was not a machine.

Day 4

George Washington

Matthew 5:16 "In the same way, let your light shine before others, so that they may see your good works and give glory to your Father in heaven."

The first president died on December 14, 1799, but news traveled slowly back then, so Methodist Bishop Francis Asbury did not find out until later and only wrote in his journal of Washington's death on January 4, 1800.

Asbury did not come right out and say, "I think Washington is in Heaven," but the preacher pretty much built the case for it. Asbury wrote, "At all times he acknowledged the providence of God, and never was he ashamed of his Redeemer: We believed he died, not fearing death."

Washington was never a Methodist, so Asbury was not trying to use Washington to provide good public relations for Asbury's church. The bishop was just giving his assessment of Washington's faith and character.

Washington was a vestryman in his church, which was kind of like being a deacon, but there were more responsibilities than a deacon typically has. Washington also insisted that Sunday services were conducted for his troops during the Revolutionary War. The first president was not perfect, but he was concerned about being a man of integrity. And Asbury knew all of that.

What will people say about our faith after we die? What will people outside of our church say about our faith? Is our witness something that comes out wherever we are, or do we confine our religious expressions to within our church walls where it is safe?

Let us pray today that we would be bold in demonstrating a Christian faith characterized by love, grace, and holiness.

Day 5

Theodore Roosevelt, William Taft

Matthew 6:12 "And forgive us our debts, as we also have forgiven our debtors."

On January 6, 1919, Teddy Roosevelt died, and William Taft cried after the funeral.

The two men had been close friends when Taft served in Roosevelt's Cabinet. They were so close, in fact, that Roosevelt endorsed Taft as his successor for the presidency.

Taft had served loyally for several years, and Roosevelt, who had become increasingly progressive (by the standards of the early 1900s), believed that Taft was the man to carry his political vision forward. Taft turned out to be quite conservative (again, by the standards of his day), and Roosevelt felt betrayed. Roosevelt was so unhappy with Taft's presidency that Roosevelt decided to run against him in the election of 1912, whereupon it was Taft who felt betrayed.

The two men split the vote sufficiently for Woodrow Wilson to win the presidency.

Fortunately, at some point before January of 1919, Taft and Roosevelt worked out their issues. Taft would say at his friend's funeral that their reconciliation brought him great peace.

Life is short. We need to forgive people. Someone who hurt you might not deserve your forgiveness. Then again, we don't deserve Christ's forgiveness, but He offers it to us anyway.

Who do we need to forgive today?

Day 6

George W. Bush

2 Timothy 1:7 "For God has not given us a spirit of fearfulness, but one of power, love, and sound judgment."

On January 6 2001, George W. Bush was finally formally certified as the winner of the Presidential Election of 2000.

Much drama had ensued beforehand. On Election Night 2000, Bush looked like he had the race won. In fact, Al Gore made the customary phone call to Bush, acknowledging the Republican's victory and offering his congratulations.

The major newspaper in Lexington, Kentucky, printed the headline "Bush Gets the W!"

Let's be honest—for newspaper humor, that wasn't bad.

But then a funny thing happened on the way to the inauguration...

There was some weirdness in Florida. Issues arose in a few voting precincts that had historically leaned hard toward the Democrats. Ballots had been filled out incorrectly. Democrats said Americans had a right for their ballots to be counted the way the voters meant for them to be counted. Less gracious folks said Bush was trying to steal the election. Republicans said we had to follow Constitutional guidelines, or no elections would ever be decided. Less gracious folks said if people were too incompetent to fill out a ballot properly, maybe they shouldn't get their votes counted.

Many opinions and rulings followed that tended to favor the politics of the person offering the opinion or ruling. But the country needed a president, and a choice had to be made, so the Supreme Court issued a decision, results were accepted, and Bush was certified.

Sometimes we just have to be bold and make a decision instead of waffling until it is too late. Let's pray for boldness today.

Day 7

Abraham Lincoln

Luke 14:28 "For which of you, wanting to build a tower, doesn't first sit down and calculate the cost to see if he has enough to complete it?"

On January 7, 1862, Lincoln wrote to Union General DC Buell, "Delay is ruining us." This was in the context of the Civil War. Lincoln's chronic problem was a shortage of generals who were willing to aggressively go after the Confederate Army. There are several maxims we can apply to warfare, and one of them should be "You can't win if you won't fight."

The Confederate generals did not suffer from the same timidity, but they were fighting for their way of life, which probably sounded more inspirational than rhetoric about "preserving the Union" or saving our "experiment in democracy," which were talking points in the North.

Certainly, there are times when caution and deliberation are important. But when it comes to our faith, there are a lot of times when we don't want to do something. We know it is wrong to say "no," so instead we say, "Not yet," or pray, "Are You *really* wanting this, Lord?" We hesitate until the opportunity is lost.

Interestingly, today's devotion and the previous one have the same theme, even though they were originally written months apart, have different Scriptures, and cite historical examples from different centuries. Sometimes we need to hear the same message more than once before we act on it.

We should pray for guidance as to what, if any, bold and decisive step we need to make in our near future.

Day 8

Bill Clinton

Psalm 51:2 "Completely wash away my guilt and cleanse me from my sin. For I am conscious of my rebellion, and my sin is always before me."

On January 7, 1999, the impeachment trial of Bill Clinton began in the US Senate. He was charged with lying under oath and obstruction of justice. These crimes were allegedly committed in an effort to hide his affair with a young intern. Ultimately, a majority of senators voted to remove the president from office, but the number fell short of the two-thirds majority needed to cost Clinton his job. Thus, he finished out his term.

Critics of the president said he disgraced the presidency. Supporters said this was much ado about nothing.

One wonders if the scandal cost Clinton's VP, Al Gore, his own opportunity at the presidency, but that is speculation best suited for another time.

How many of us have heard someone say about a person who did something wrong, "Is he sorry he did it, or is he sorry he got caught?"

When we are caught in our sins, are we ashamed that we fell short and now repentant, or are we embarrassed that now people know who we really are? Is our temptation to lie and try to cover up our sin, or are we willing to ask the Lord to renew a right spirit in us?

Are we willing to own our baggage? Today could be the day.

Day 9

Abraham Lincoln

Matthew 7:12 "Therefore, whatever you want others to do for you, do also the same for them, for this is the Law and the Prophets."

On January 10, 1862, Trusten Polk was kicked out of the United States Senate for disloyalty. He was a southern sympathizer during the Civil War. Earlier, he had publicly criticized Lincoln over the Republican's handling of the crisis at Fort Sumter and the start of the Civil War.

Trusten Polk was the third cousin once removed of James K. Polk. When Lincoln was a member of the House of Representatives, Lincoln criticized James Polk for his actions leading up to the Mexican War. When Lincoln had his own war to manage, a Polk in the government criticized him.

A Polk partisan might call that poetic justice.

A Lincoln lover might say this is comparing an apple to an orange.

This reminds me of the old saying, "What goes around, comes around." In other words, sometimes we get what we dish out, which is a fairly decent incentive to live out the Golden Rule.

Given this reality, maybe we should communicate love and encouragement. There are times when strong and blunt words are needed, but some of us do not confine ourselves to those rare occasions.

We should ask the Lord who we need to build up and encourage today.

Day 10

Ronald Reagan

Galatians 5:22-23 "But the fruit of the Spirit is love, joy, peace, patience, kindness, goodness, faithfulness, gentleness, and self-control. The law is not against such things."

Martin Luther King Jr. was born on January 15, 1929. In 1983, Ronald Reagan signed a bill into law that created a holiday on the third Monday of January to celebrate Reverend King. It is between January 15 and 21 each year.

Proponents: He brought America closer to living up to its reputation for liberty, justice, and opportunity.

Critics (who have dwindled greatly over the years, according to my anecdotal and completely unscientific research): All the presidents in American history (but mostly Washington and Lincoln) have to share a day (when we don't even close most of our businesses), and MLK gets a day all to himself?

The point here: The nation has changed when it comes to the conversation about race. I met a woman who was 14 in 1980 when Reagan got elected, and she was convinced back then that the new president was going to send all African Americans to Africa. Obviously, he didn't.

If the nation can change and grow, why can't we? Has racism left the church? Not entirely. Is it possible that some people reading this book have a little soul-searching to do today when it comes to racial attitudes and behaviors? It might be more than just possible.

Day 11

Abraham Lincoln

Colossians 3:13 "Bearing with one another and forgiving one another if anyone has a grievance against another. Just as the Lord has forgiven you, so you are also to forgive."

On January 17 in 1851, Thomas Lincoln died. His son, Abraham, did not bother to attend the funeral. In fact, the elder Lincoln never met his son's wife or the children of Abraham and Mary Lincoln. Abraham had a rough and sad childhood, and he never forgave his father.

This wasn't the age of tell-all books, so we don't know exactly what transpired between the Lincoln men. Abraham's mother died when Lincoln was a child, and his father abandoned him and his sister temporarily as he traveled out of state to bring back a woman he knew. She was his new wife.

Those were practical times, if not particularly romantic ones.

Was Abraham angry at being left alone? Was his father guilty of other sins and shortcomings? Probably. And maybe cutting his father out of his life was nothing other than an effort by the future 16th president to keep his wife and children safe from a bad man.

It certainly seems reasonable to believe there was a lack of forgiveness on Lincoln's part.

The death of any parent is a tragedy. There's either the loss of a special and unique relationship, or there is an end to a relationship that will now never be what it could have been. Either way, our faith is based on forgiveness. If we can't forgive the ones who've hurt us, then some of our wounds will NEVER heal.

If this is a burden you have been carrying, pray for the strength to forgive someone who hurt you. If you know of someone else who is struggling to forgive, take a moment and say a prayer for them.

Day 12

George HW Bush

Proverbs 11:13 "A gossip goes around revealing a secret, but a trustworthy person keeps a confidence."

George Herbert Walker Bush held many important jobs in addition to being President of the United States. His last day at one such job was January 20, 1977, when he stepped down as Director of the CIA. Whatever one might think about the CIA—it's wonderful/it's a necessary evil/it's just another arm of foreign relations/it's horrible—I imagine we all agree that an important attribute of someone in the Director's chair is being able to keep secrets.

The Republican Bush gave up this job after a Democrat, Jimmy Carter, captured the White House, but Bush was able to build on his success as CIA director, and his other positions, and become vice president just four years later. This set him up for his successful run for the White House.

Are we people of integrity? Can we be trusted to protect someone's confidential information? Do we gossip, or are we sensitive?

A great way for us to lose people's respect is to share information that we shouldn't.

Ben Franklin once said, "The only way for three people to keep a secret is if two of them are dead."

Fortunately, that is not always true.

We can be trustworthy. We need to be trustworthy as believers. Praying to be trustworthy would be a worthwhile thing to do today.

Day 13

William McKinley

Genesis 2:24 "This is why a man leaves his father and mother and bonds with his wife, and they become one flesh."

On January 25, 1871, William McKinley entered into wedded bliss with Ida Saxton. It might not have been a romance for the ages, but they were close to one another. Ida had some health challenges, but the president doted on her.

McKinley won the presidency primarily because the economy was terrible when the opposition party, the Democrats, held the White House, but it also helped that he had a reputation as an honest man and a loving husband of a sick wife.

The quality of our marriages says something about us. It is a part of our witness. Parents don't just raise their kids; parents model for them what marriage looks like.

How we treat our spouses, and the things we say about them behind their backs, can be a witness to nonbelievers.

Hurtful jokes, cutting remarks, and selfish behavior not only bring our spouses down, they also trash our witness.

The exact opposite is also true. Cherishing our spouses doesn't just elevate their spirits; it can also point people toward Christ.

Of course, marriage is not always easy. Ida McKinley had physical problems, and her husband was distracted by his political career. But they figured out how to make it work.

We don't need to be married in order to respect and support the institution. We should today pray for our own marriages, if applicable, and for the married people closest to us—pray that they cherish one another.

Day 14

Jimmy Carter

I Corinthians 10:31 "So, whether you eat or drink or whatever you do, do everything for the glory of God."

On January 27,1900, Admiral Hyman G. Rickover was born. He became a driving force behind America's nuclear submarine program, and he was a mentor of a young naval officer named Jimmy Carter.

"Why not the best?" Rickover liked to ask his people. If someone was going to do, well, anything; why would that person do less than their best?

This idea had a huge impact on the trajectory of Jimmy Carter's life. He committed himself to doing his best, and this mentality led him to become Governor of Georgia and eventually President of the United States.

His time in the White House was not remembered kindly by the majority of Americans who voted him out after four years, but Carter's philosophy of doing his best turned out pretty good overall—at least it got him to the presidency.

Most of us have cut corners when it comes to doing our best. In our workplaces, in our families, and when it comes to the Kingdom of God, most of us do not always give our top effort. The root of our problem might be lust, insecurity, sloth, or simply the distraction of our phones, but we have given Christ and others less than our best.

This devotion is not meant to make you feel bad about a past that you can't change; this is about praying for God's strength to be the disciple, family member, friend, employee, or boss that God wants you to be. Let's pray for that today.

Day 15

Millard Fillmore

Psalm 73:1 "God is indeed good to Israel, to the pure in heart."

In the mid-1800s, people were moving west in large numbers. The USA was growing fast, and much like today, there was a lot of debate over who and what we should be as a country.

On January 29, 1850, Millard Fillmore signed legislation known as the "Compromise of 1850." There were several parts to this, but two of the biggest were that California came into the Union as a free state, which pleased the North, and there was a new, and tougher, Fugitive Slave Act, which made the South happy.

The series of compromises didn't please everybody, of course, because, well, they were a bunch of compromises. But Fillmore was pretty happy. He said the agreement would "restore compromise and peace to our distracted country." Ten years later, states began leaving the Union, and soon after, the Civil War began.

Sometimes compromises are important and necessary, especially in a democracy. But there are also principles that Christians should not be willing to back away from.

Do we, in our desire to be popular or at least to get along with people, compromise on Biblical truth?

A wise man named Joseph North said to me shortly before I wrote this entry, "You can't have true love without truth and love. One or the other isn't enough."

Is there an area of our lives where we need to stand our ground in order to be pure in heart? We need to do that in love, not hate, but we need to do that.

Day 16

Thomas Jefferson

Psalm 26:4 "I do not sit with the worthless or associate with hypocrites."

A letter dated January 30, 1787, was sent from Thomas Jefferson to his friend James Madison. Jefferson, ever the colorful wordsmith, wrote "The tree of liberty must be refreshed from time to time with the blood of patriots and tyrants." This line is often quoted, both because it communicates the important truth that freedom is usually won at a great price, and because it sounds so eloquent.

The next line is typically left out. "It is its natural manure."

The line is seldom included because comparing the blood of patriots to manure is decidedly not eloquent, yet Jefferson is accurately pointing out that both military sacrifice and fertilizer lead to life.

The second line is included in today's devotional, and it's not the only thing that stinks here. Jefferson might have casually written about other people dying for freedom, but he wasn't so casual about dying himself. Washington fought in the Revolution, Adams was too old, Madison tried to join the military years before the war but was too sickly, Monroe fought, John Quincy Adams was too young, and Andrew Jackson was too young but fought anyway, because he's Andrew Jackson.

What of Jefferson?

But this book is not about military careers; it's about being Christian disciples. Are we people who believe in the cause of Christians sharing their faith with those who need to hear, yet guilty of never personally sharing our faith? If I say I believe the Bible, but I don't ever share my faith, (I know this will sound harsh but) I'm not a witness; I'm a hypocrite.

Let's be something better than hypocrites today.

Day 17

Martin Van Buren

1 Corinthians 13:12 "For now we see only a reflection as in a mirror, but then face to face. Now I know in part, but then I will know fully, as I am fully known."

On February 5, 1819, Hannah Hoes Van Buren died at the tender age of 35. In Martin Van Buren's 776-page autobiography, published two years before he was elected president, he doesn't mention his wife.

It might seem strange that a man would write an autobiography before his presidency, but Van Buren is not the only world leader to do that kind of thing. At least in Van Buren's case, he had been involved in party politics for years, then served as secretary of state and vice president, so he had interesting stories he could tell.

Still, 776 is a lot of pages.

And not mentioning his wife in his book? That is definitely strange. Was she really shy, and he wanted to respect that? Did they have a terrible marriage? Had he neglected her to the point that after her death, he felt too guilty to write about that aspect of his life? We don't know, because he didn't write about her.

If he did not want to share anything about his wife, should we respect his privacy? On the other hand, if a guy spends his career in national politics and writes a 776-page autobiography, can he really complain about a lack of privacy?

Today, we have lots of questions and no answers. What is the takeaway here? It's this: There are mysteries in this life that we will never get answers to, and we need to be okay with that. We don't need to have everything figured out, because God is in control.

Day 18

Richard Nixon

Exodus 32:4 "He took the gold from them, fashioned it with an engraving tool, and made it into the image of a calf."

On February 8, 2019, I appeared on a local TV show to talk about my book *Presidential Stories,* and I mentioned (among other things) that Richard Nixon was incredibly awkward in his social interactions. As I was preparing for the segment, I thought about a story I did not tell that day. One time Nixon showed up for a photo shoot, and his clothes were so ridiculous that people laughed at him. Then I thought about how my friends laughed at me for wearing clothes that didn't fit the occasion. You shouldn't wear cargo shorts to work out at the gym? Where is that written down? How do people just automatically know that? My point is that I can relate to Nixon (at least to a degree), and because of that, I can learn from him.

And so it is with Aaron and the golden calf. When I was a kid, I thought it was, well, dumb that the Israelites would make a golden calf and then worship it like a god. Later, one of my professors in grad school explained that the golden calf was created to draw out a local god or gods who would come down and be worshipped. The Israelites weren't worshipping the calf; they wanted to worship whichever invisible deity would come down and sit on the calf.

The Israelites thought their God was confined to the mountain with Moses, so they were trying to control Him or get help elsewhere.

We can't really relate to people who worship a golden calf, but we can learn from people who are willing to put their faith in something less than God, because we have done that.

We need to take the time to try and understand people, so we can learn from their victories *and* their mistakes. Some of us need to strive to be less dismissive of others today.

Day 19

Barack Obama

Matthew 6:14 "For if you forgive others their offenses, your heavenly Father will forgive you as well."

On February 8, 2007, Joe Biden got himself in some hot water by saying in reference to Barack Obama, "I mean, you got the first mainstream African American who is articulate and bright and clean and a nice-looking guy. I mean, that's a storybook, man."

Many people wondered if the future president took offense at Biden's words. I would think the most offended parties would be the African Americans who ran before Obama. Still, to refer to an articulate and nice-looking African American as something out of a storybook, well, that could certainly be considered condescending.

Or worse.

The future president saved Biden from a lot of grief when Obama publicly said it was no big deal and he wasn't offended by his fellow Democrat. Obama later doubled down on the forgiveness thing when he picked Biden as his VP.

What about us? Has someone done something in our lives that might label him/her as a possible enemy? What if we responded with forgiveness and grace? What a powerful testimony that would be. To whom in our lives could we show grace today?

Day 20

John Tyler

Matthew 6:5A "Whenever you pray, you must not be like the hypocrites."

While serving as a US senator for the fine state of Virginia, John Tyler gave an interesting speech.[1] Okay, actually the topic of the speech was not that interesting. It was about tariffs. But he said something that caught my attention. Tyler said he had a vision of the United States "overturning the strong places of despotism and restoring to man his long-lost rights."

It was not exactly unique that an early American would see something special about our freedom-loving country, or cast us in the role of an example or a champion for the rest of the world. What is interesting is that while Tyler romanticized about restoring rights to others, he personally deprived people of their rights who lived on his plantation. Some of our Founding Fathers owned slaves, but typically they saw that slavery was incompatible with liberty. They grew to hate slavery, and while they did not end it, many of them chipped away at the institution to a limited degree.

Tyler, and many other slave-owning politicians who succeeded the Founders, did not chip away at slavery. Tyler defended it, and as president, he surrounded himself with like-minded, slave-owning advisors. Then despite having been President of the United States, Tyler supported the Confederacy, as a way of holding onto the southern way of life, which included slavery.

John Tyler was a hypocrite.

I do not write this to mock him; I want to turn the light on us. What are our blind spots? Is there an area of our lives where we are inconsistent and hypocritical? Today, let's pray that God would open our eyes to the inconsistencies in our own walk and witness.

---

[1] It was February 8, sometime in the 1820s-1830s.

Day 21

Andrew Johnson

Ezekiel 13:9A "My hand will be against the prophets who see false visions and speak lying divinations."

Andrew Johnson had a little drama added to his life in 1869. Presidential inaugurations took place in March in the 1800s, so Johnson was in his final weeks in the White House on February 10, but he was not leaving soon enough for Annie O'Neil. She got arrested while brandishing a pistol and saying she was "sent by God Almighty" to kill Johnson.

There was a time when it was popular in some Christian circles to share one's faith by saying what God had done in one's life, because, the argument went, "No one can say God didn't do something in your life, if you know He did it."

That rationale seemed flawed to me, and Annie O'Neil demonstrates what that flaw was. I am quite comfortable saying God did not tell her to murder the president. She said God told her to do it, but, well, she's wrong.

History has plenty of examples of people blaming their wrong behavior on God's will. What about us? Do we have trouble separating our agenda from God's? How many teenagers have pulled the plug on a relationship by saying, "I prayed about this, and God doesn't want me to date you anymore"? How many of us non teenagers have failed to do our Christian duty with the excuse of, "Well, God hasn't given me a burden for that"? When God's Word tells us what His will is, do we expect Him to also whisper instructions in our ear?

We need to stop blaming God for our sins of commission as well as our sins of omission.

Day 22

Theodore Roosevelt

1 Thessalonians 4:13 "We do not want you to be uninformed, brothers and sisters, concerning those who are asleep, so that you will not grieve like the rest, who have no hope."

The first volume of this series, entitled *Presidential* Stories, included the tale of something terrible that happened on February 14, 1884—the day Theodore Roosevelt lost both his wife and his mother. What I didn't mention in that book was his conscious decision to bury the pain of his loss. He reasoned that if he buried it, then it would not impact his day to day life moving forward.

Grief is a normal process. We should not feel the need to hide it.

Or hide from it.

On an extremely personal note, I started working on this entry early in 2019. On the morning of May 12, 2019, my wife died suddenly and unexpectedly. My understanding of grief grew exponentially.

In the sixteen years and nine months I was married to Angela, I believe I cried five times. I wept during a funeral service, and I cried over the news of a nephew with a brain tumor (he's better now), I cried during an episode of *The Flash* (okay, that one surprised me, but in my defense, it was a very moving episode), and there were a couple of other occasions.

In the three months after Angela died, I cried every day, multiple times a day. Letting the grief out, praying, choosing joy, and talking to people when I needed to all helped me make my way forward.

If you are grieving, it can get better. If you know someone who is grieving, tell them you love them. It helps.

Day 23

Franklin Roosevelt

Deuteronomy 31:6 "Be strong and courageous; don't be terrified or afraid of them. For the Lord your God is the One who will go with you; He will not leave you or abandon you."

When Pearl Harbor fell victim to a sneak attack by the Japanese in 1941, many Americans were afraid of what might happen next. Would there be further attacks? Would we lose Hawaii?

What kind of danger was posed by "those people" who were living in the continental United States?

To deal with this perceived threat, on February 19, 1942, Franklin Roosevelt signed Executive Order 9066. It authorized the relocation and internment of people of Japanese ancestry living in the United States. It was an obviously unconstitutional thing to do—pulling people away from their homes and jobs, and sticking them in camps, not because they had done anything wrong, but simply because of their ethnicity.

Eleanor Roosevelt was shocked and upset by her husband's decision, and she let him know it. The Roosevelts did not have the greatest marriage in the history of the presidency—the president was an adulterer—but he did respect his wife's intelligence and political savvy. Nevertheless, he ordered the violation of the rights of Japanese Americans anyway.

When we are scared, we are vulnerable to bad decision-making. One way to guard against this is to listen to people close to us. Franklin Roosevelt ignored a voice of reason and fairness. Perhaps today we are wrestling with a decision, and we would do well to learn from his mistake. Perhaps today we need to seek godly counsel, and not give in to a spirit of fear.

Day 24

George Washington

Hebrews 13:8 "Jesus Christ is the same yesterday, today, and forever."

The first president was born on February 22, 1732. (Actually, they didn't consider it a February 22 birthday at the time, but there was an adjustment made to the calendar, and, um, never mind.)

In the year 1885, the federal government passed a law making Washington's birthday one of just four federal holidays. The others were Christmas, Thanksgiving, and July 4. (Easter is always on Sundays, so offices were already closed anyway.)

Years later, the February holiday was tweaked so that the date would float around a little bit, and it would also include Abraham Lincoln.

My point is that George Washington, who died in 1799, was hugely popular throughout the 1800s. What he did for the United States of America is uniquely significant.

Washington is not really celebrated as much these days. In fact, in the 1990s, there was a movement to remove his name from many of the public schools named after him, based on the argument that he was just another dead slave owner.

Public opinion had changed from overwhelming bipartisan love for Washington to something less than that. It's an interesting lesson on how vulnerable we are if we try to please other people. Not only might their perceptions be unfair, but their opinions can change even when we don't.

Maybe we should instead strive to please the One who is the same yesterday, today, and forever. Let us pray that we might please the Lord today.

Day 25

Jimmy Carter

Matthew 5:16 "In the same way, let your light shine before others, so that they may see your good works and give glory to your Father in heaven."

I was in a preaching class offered by my church, and my assignment on February 24, 2019, was to speak on a random topic thrown out by someone in the room. My friend Travis Gordon, suggested I "talk about a president whose faith impacted his job."

The first president to come to mind was Jimmy Carter. Overall, President Carter's time in office would be hard to characterize as successful. He had trouble navigating the Iran hostage crisis, and the economy was pretty bad. While presidents usually get too much blame when the economy hits a rough patch, Carter has been criticized by some for leadership that was rather uninspiring.

That said, there were a couple of areas where Carter truly shined. One of them was character. After Johnson's lies regarding the Vietnam War, and Nixon's lies over that war and Watergate, it was easy to be cynical about the White House. Could anyone do the job anymore without being a self-serving liar?

Carter built his campaign around the idea that he answered to God for his behavior, so he needed to be a man of integrity. He talked about being "born again," and he promised he would never lie to the American people. There were those, including his own mother, who thought this was an unrealistic expectation. But many people who weren't fans of his job performance at least recognized that he truly was a man of genuine character.

Sometimes it's tough to be a person of integrity, but if we can demonstrate Christian character in such circumstances, our light for Christ will shine all that much brighter than it would ordinarily. We should let our light shine today.

Day 26

Benjamin Harrison

Ephesians 6:18 "Pray at all times in the Spirit with every prayer and request, and stay alert with all perseverance and intercession for all the saints."

Benjamin Harrison is one of the more obscure presidents in American history. If people know anything about him at all, it is probably just that he and his grandfather, William Henry Harrison, are the only grandson-grandfather duo of presidents in American History. If people know anything else about Benjamin Harrison, it is probably that he was president between the two terms of Grover Cleveland.

Yet Harrison is worth knowing because he is a good role model for us.

On February 25, 1789, Harrison led his family in prayer before departing from home and heading off to Washington DC. Someone present for the big goodbye remarked that Harrison always knew what to say when it came to speeches and prayers. So, now we know that about president #23—he was a man of eloquent prayers.

Would people say that about us? Do people know that we pray at all? It's not that eloquence or public opinion matters when it comes to prayers, but these things can be fruit of the vine. What about the vine (praying) itself?

Do we pray?

Do we pray like we should (thoughtfully and constantly)? Let's pray this way today.

Day 27

Theodore Roosevelt

Philippians 2:14 "Do everything without grumbling or arguing."

On February 28, 2019, my wife showed me a quotation from Theodore Roosevelt: "Complaining about a problem without posing a solution is called whining."

She found it on the internet, which begs the question, "Is this any more reliable than that quotation that was all over social media a while back, saying, 'More than half of all the quotations on the internet are made up'?" That one is attributed to Abraham Lincoln.

The Roosevelt quotation is a little more reliable than that, but some people still raise an eyebrow at it.

Whether or not Roosevelt actually said what was attributed to him here is beside my point—it is still a great line.

In church, at work, and with our family or friends, are we solution-oriented, or are we chronic complainers? Do we lack the joy of the Lord and the confidence we are offered as his children? If we are constantly bemoaning the negative, what does that do to our witness?

The answer: nothing good.

We have the ultimate solution for the problems of the world: Jesus. People might be more likely to listen to that solution if we are already offering them words of hope and encouragement, rather than the chronic negativity that some of us default toward.

Day 28

Thomas Jefferson and James Madison

Luke 16:8A "The master praised the unrighteous manager because he had acted shrewdly."

On March 3, 1801, the Alien and Sedition Acts expired, thus ending a frustrating episode in the lives of Jefferson and Madison.

Their issue: Congress had passed a series of acts in 1798 designed to stop Jefferson's party, the Democratic-Republicans, from complaining about the Federalists' foreign policy.

This was a clear violation of the First Amendment-protected right of free speech. The problem was that the Federalists controlled the White House, Congress, and the Supreme Court. How could Jefferson and Madison oppose this unconstitutional legislation? They hadn't fought in the last war, so there was no way they were going to take up arms over this.

What could they do? Seriously, what do you think they did? My students are stumped by this question every semester. The answer: Jefferson and Madison attacked the laws in the state legislatures of Virginia and Kentucky. Wasn't that creative?

In the November 1800 elections, the voters protected the Constitution by voting out many Federalists and putting the other party in control of Congress and the White House.

The question for today, though, is how creative are we when it comes to living out our Christian walk? How do we maintain our moral standards when we work for an unethical boss? How do we share Christ when the conversation feels awkward to us? Do we look for creative solutions, or do we just throw up our hands? Jefferson and Madison thought outside the box. Their solution did not solve their problem, but at least they didn't quit on it. They kept trying, and the problem took care of itself. What if sometimes God wants to see us try, and then He will intervene? Let's be doers.

Day 29

Grover Cleveland

Galatians 3:13-14 "Christ redeemed us from the curse of the law by becoming a curse for us, because it is written, 'Cursed is everyone who is hung on a tree.' The purpose was that the blessing of Abraham would come to the Gentiles by Christ Jesus."

On March 3, 1863, Congress passed, and Lincoln signed into law, the Enrollment Act, which established a draft in the Union during the Civil War.

Five future presidents served in this war. It would have been six, but Grover Cleveland took advantage of a clause in the law that allowed him to hire a replacement to serve in his place. Thus, a Polish immigrant went and fought, and Cleveland avoided service.

For some things in life, the price just seems too high. Such was the case for Grover Cleveland and military service in wartime. Part of me wants to criticize the guy, but I never served, so I don't have the right to be an armchair warrior.

My point for the day is actually this: There was a price that was too high for us to pay even if we wanted to. I'm talking about the price that we owe because of our sin.

Jesus paid that price. If you are reading this book and you made it to Day 29, you most likely already know this truth, but let's live today like we are truly thankful for it.

Day 30

Abraham Lincoln

Genesis 3:12-13 "The man replied, 'The woman you gave to be with me—she gave me some fruit from the tree, and I ate.'
So the Lord God asked the woman, 'What is this you have done?'
And the woman said, 'The serpent deceived me, and I ate.'"

On March 4, 1861, Abraham Lincoln was inaugurated as President of the United States. Immediately, he had to figure out what to do with the Confederate blockade of the Union held Fort Sumter, located in South Carolina.

James Buchanan had done nothing to deal with the problem, but Lincoln never publicly complained about or blamed Buchanan. On the one hand it wasn't really Buchanan's fault that the South seceded. Southern states had pledged to leave the Union if a Republican got elected president, and Buchanan was a Democrat.

On the other hand, the election took place in November, and the inauguration would not be until the day mentioned above, March 4. Buchanan had four months to try something. He called for a day of prayer in January, and that was nice, but he did not consult with the incoming president about what to do, nor did Buchanan act unilaterally to try to stop secession before it got out of control.

Even if it wasn't fair to blame Buchanan, and many historians are quite comfortable pointing their fingers at him, it would not have been Lincoln's worst move politically. He certainly could have taken some political pressure off himself if he had said, "It is too late to fix this because Buchanan squandered so much time." But Lincoln didn't waste time casting blame; he just focused on the solution.

How many of us are quick to deflect responsibility in times of trouble? Let us pray for the fortitude to be solution-oriented instead of blame-oriented.

Day 31

Richard Nixon

1 Corinthians 15:33 "Do not be deceived: bad company corrupts good morals."

On March 4, 1974, Chuck Colson and six other men were indicted on crimes related to the Watergate investigations.

How did so many successful men get caught up in such corruption? Colson would later point out that, basically, everybody wanted to be Daddy's favorite. In this case, Richard Nixon was Daddy, and his personality was such that it was really hard to get close to him. But Nixon valued winning; he liked people who got the job done. Thus, some of his people reached the point where they would do anything to succeed and please the boss. And they started crossing lines.

Who are we trying to please? As Christians, we would say "God." But…who else? Are we trying to please an unethical employer or mean friends we are afraid of challenging? Are we trying to be friends with our kids instead of their parents? Are we trying to placate a difficult spouse? Do we compromise our values in order to be successful, win approval, or just avoid trouble?

We need to pray for strength. And maybe we need to pray for better company (though, let me be clear, this is not a justification for divorce).

Day 32

Ulysses Grant

Matthew 25:24-27 "The man who had received one talent also approached and said, 'Master, I know you. You're a harsh man, reaping where you haven't sown and gathering where you haven't scattered seed. So I was afraid and went off and hid your talent in the ground. See, you have what is yours.'

His master replied to him, 'You evil, lazy servant! If you knew that I reap where I haven't sown and gather where I haven't scattered, then you should have deposited my money with the bankers, and I would have received my money back with interest when I returned.'"

Ulysses Grant became the Commander in Chief of Union forces in the Civil War on March 9, 1863. Grant could have gotten his feelings hurt that it took Lincoln two years into the war to give Grant this opportunity. The general could have decided that since the Union had squandered its advantages for those two years the job was too hard.

Grant could have looked at his past failures in life and decided the responsibility was too big for him. He could have noted how many commanders had been reassigned by Lincoln, and Grant could have decided to avoid the potential humiliation of another failure.

Instead, Grant accepted the assignment, dug in his heels, and over the next two years defeated the Confederates and brought the war to an end.

What task of the Lord have we refused because it seemed like we were unappreciated by somebody, it was too hard, we felt too unworthy, or a combination thereof? God gives us talents, passions, and opportunities. We need to not squander them; we need to prayerfully figure out how to be the best stewards we can possibly be.

Day 33

Franklin Roosevelt

Proverbs 22:29 "Do you see a person skilled in his work? He will stand in the presence of kings. He will not stand in the presence of the unknown."

World War Two had been raging in Europe for a little over a year in a half when on March 11, 1941 Franklin D. Roosevelt signed the Lend Lease Act. This new law authorized the president to make deals with foreign powers without the approval of the Senate. Basically, this empowered the president to sell, loan, or trade war materials to the Allies.

Part of what made all of this so dramatic was that just a few years earlier, Congress had passed a series of Neutrality Acts, which put in place a number of restrictions on trade. Congress did not want US trade policy to favor one side over the other, which is what we did in World War One. The rationale was that picking a side ultimately dragged us into a war that left 100,000 Americans dead. Here we were again, facing a bigger, badder world war only twenty years removed from fighting the War to End All Wars.

FDR rationalized Lend Lease by saying this wouldn't drag us into the war. No, we would become the arsenal of freedom. The Allies would stop the war over there before we had to face it over here.

US trade policy shifted dramatically in just a few short years, because the Fascists were a bigger threat than the world faced in World War One. FDR and Congress realized they couldn't use yesterday's solutions for today's problems.

We need to realize that, too, whether the issue is how to do evangelism, how to do discipleship, how to face challenges at work, or how to raise the kids. We need to be open to prayerfully considering new solutions today.

Day 34

Andrew Jackson

2 Timothy 1:7 "For God has not given us a spirit of fearfulness, but one of power, love, and sound judgment."

On March 15, 1767, Andrew Jackson was born. What makes his birthdate significant is it shows how young he was when the Revolutionary War happened. The fighting in this struggle for independence lasted from 1775-1781.

Undeterred by his youth, Jackson got involved in the war effort, which led to his capture as a 13-year-old.

When a Redcoat demanded that the young prisoner make himself useful by shining the officer's boots, Jackson refused. He got smacked with the flat side of a sword for his insolence, but he never did shine that fancy footwear.

Bravery has a cost—Jackson earned a permanent scar on his face.

Bravery carries a reward, too. Jackson was quite proud of that scar There is satisfaction in doing the right thing, even when it is not easy. As Christians, we are challenged in Scripture to not follow the path of least resistance. Timid people usually don't change the world, and our lost world needs a change. Let's pray for that spirit of power that Paul talks about.

Day 35

Abraham Lincoln

Psalm 27:1 "The Lord is my light and my salvation. Whom shall I fear? The Lord is the stronghold of my life. Whom shall I dread?"

On March 17, 2019, I asked my pastor, Dr. John Green IV, to tell me a president he admired and why. Was it a shameless and contrived effort to get content for today?

Well…yes.

He is a wise man, though, so I was confident he would give me gold.

He picked Abraham Lincoln, because Lincoln would make tough decisions. This reminded me of a talk a general gave a few years ago in a class at Carson-Newman University. The general said that one can reach a point in leadership where the decision to choose between good and bad options is no longer available because the decisions with an obviously good choice on the table have already been made by someone of lesser authority. The hard decisions get pushed upstairs. Some leaders are constantly choosing between bad options all day long.

Many of us struggle to make hard or unpopular decisions. As a result, we let trouble fester in our homes, jobs, and churches. Sometimes the easy way is not available.

What problem do we need to confront today? Let us pray for the resolve to do what we have known for a while we need to do. Let us pray for the bravery to make a tough decision.

Day 36

William McKinley

1 Peter 4:10 "Just as each one has received a gift, use it to serve others, as good stewards of the varied grace of God."

William Jennings Bryan ran against William McKinley in the Election of 1896, and Bryan gave McKinley a serious run for his money. McKinley had what looked like insurmountable advantages, but he almost got, um, surmounted anyway. The country was going through one of the worst depressions in American history starting in the early 1890s, and the Democrats were holding the White House at the time. This made McKinley, a Republican, look like an intriguing alternative. The economy was terrible, and Democrats were badly divided on how to fix it. They were even quite splintered on who their candidate should be until Bryan rose to the top. Besides all of this, McKinley had a massively greater amount of campaign funds upon which to draw.

So, how did Bryan, born on March 19, 1860, almost come away with the victory? He was an incredible public speaker, and he was more than willing to use his gift. He did not quit even though the deck was stacked against him. He did not complain despite lacking the resources McKinley had. Bryan just focused on what he could do, and he made the best of it.

Bryan never became president, but he was picked by the Democrats to represent them in three presidential elections. And he did hold the highly influential position of secretary of state under Woodrow Wilson.

What about us? Are we making the most of what God has given us? Perhaps we don't always get what we want, but when we're good stewards of what God has blessed us with, the outcome might surprise us.

Day 37

George W. Bush

Philippians 1:9 "And I pray this: that your love will keep on growing in knowledge and every kind of discernment."

On March 20, 2019, George W. Bush did something he had never done before. The 72-year-old former president hit a hole in one on the par 3 12th hole of the Trinity Forest Golf Club.

One can only wonder how many times the president dreamed of such a shot. If his goal in playing golf was to hit a hole in one, surely he would have given up on it by age 72. What are the odds that he was thinking, "I know I have been zero for my first 71 years, but at 72, I just have a feeling—this year is going to be different"?

The man kept playing his game, and finally the ball went straight in the hole on the first shot off the tee.

What about us when it comes to ministry? It is good to have a plan, and it is good to dream big, but are we tempted to give up when we try to do something for the Lord and we don't see huge results?

We need to stop periodically and examine what we are doing. If the results aren't there, we might need to make a change. And yet there are also times when the Lord would have us persevere, and if we do, we get to see something truly remarkable happen.

All of this begs the question, "How do we know when to change course and when to stay the course?"

In our prayer time today, let's pray for discernment. Let's pray for the Lord's direction instead of relying on our moods and desire for convenience.

Day 38

John Tyler

Colossians 3:12 "Therefore, as God's chosen ones, holy and dearly loved, put on compassion, kindness, humility, gentleness, and patience."

John Tyler, born on March 29, 1790, was the first man to take office as the result of the death of a president.

His own Whig Party turned on him pretty quickly, because he had more in common with the Democrats than the Whigs. He had actually been a Democrat and had only switched parties because he hated Andrew Jackson.

Because of Tyler's political philosophy and a less-than-charismatic personality, he became the target for some hostility. At least one politician referred to him as "the Acting President," meaning that politician saw Tyler as something less than a real president.

When Tyler wanted a new presidential carriage, he got it, but he wasn't satisfied. Allegedly, he said, "This is a secondhand carriage." And he was told, "But aren't you a secondhand president?"

I don't trust this story, because I can't believe someone who worked for the White House would think he could say that and still keep his job, but the fact that the story got circulated says something about how people felt toward Tyler.

He was unpleasant, and he had an ego. Do we ever come across like we have ego problems? Do we ever act arrogant or entitled? Do we think some jobs and people are beneath us? Do we treat people as if they are not worthy of our notice? This is not indicative of an attitude or behavior appropriate for a Christ-follower. Let us pray for humility as we approach our day.

Day 39

Richard Nixon

Isaiah 40:31 "But those who trust in the Lord will renew their strength; they will soar on wings like eagles; they will run and not become weary, they will walk and not faint."

On April Fools' Day in 1970, Richard Nixon signed into law a bill called "The Public Health Cigarette Smoking Act." This new law banned cigarette ads.

Years earlier, at least one tobacco company advertised a health benefit to smoking: stress relief. Seriously. The ad featured a number of baseball players from a World Series winning team who smoked. The tobacco company took credit for the players' ability to perform well in a pressure-packed situation.

In 1964, there was a Surgeon General's warning about the harmful side effects of cigarettes, and then things began to change.

What is there in our lives that is unhealthy for us spiritually, yet we argue just the opposite?

Bible-believing, churchgoing married people get tempted by someone who is not their spouse, but these married folks tell themselves it's okay because God wants them to be happy.

Too many of us eat much more than we need to, and then laugh nervously at Scripture passages about gluttony, because it feels easier to find peace in comfort food than it does to wait on the Prince of Peace.

Too many of us use alcohol or some not-so-legal drug to numb us to the pains of this life.

For those who are struggling today, wait on the Lord. For those who are not, pray for the opportunity to use today's Scripture to encourage someone else.

Day 40

William Henry Harrison

Genesis 12:1 "The Lord said to Abram, 'Go out from your land, your relatives, and your father's house to the land that I will show you.'"

William Henry Harrison wasn't president for very long. When he died on April 4, 1841, he had only been in office a month. But to get the job, he did a couple of things that were quite innovative. He campaigned personally. A presidential candidate going around giving speeches and asking for votes was quite the rarity before the 1900s. There might have only been two other men who tried this in the 1800s—William Jennings Bryan (who was mentioned on Day 36) and Stephen Douglas (who ran against Abe Lincoln in 1860), and both of them lost.

Thus, one could argue that Harrison was ahead of his time.

He also had the first campaign slogan: "Tippecanoe and Tyler Too." Harrison had become famous by leading American troops in military actions against the Native Americans. The Battle of Tippecanoe was an important victory Harrison won in 1811. By reminding voters of Harrison's exploits, the Whig Party easily evoked comparisons to George Washington and Andrew Jackson, both popular and successful generals who went on to become popular and successful presidents.

When we want to have an impact, sometimes we have to do what others have not done before. Obviously, if we are blazing a new trail where there is no map, then we won't have a clear path. We have an opportunity to exercise our faith. We need to pray beforehand and ask for guidance, and then pray through the process.

It's easier to play it safe, but that is often not our calling. We might need to start on a journey today before the Lord shows us the destination. Are we open to such a journey?

Day 41

Donald Trump

2 Timothy 3:16-17 "All Scripture is inspired by God and is profitable for teaching, for rebuking, for correcting, for training in righteousness, so that the man of God may be complete, equipped for every good work."

On April 4, 2019, there were several stories on the Internet about sportswriter Rick Reilly's new book, *Commander in Cheat*, which detailed the 45th president's alleged propensity for taking unfair advantage in otherwise friendly games of golf.

Human nature being what it is, many people who like Trump either chose to disbelieve the stories based on the headlines alone, or they argued that how he plays golf doesn't really impact his policy positions as president.

Human nature being what it is, many people who don't like Trump chose to believe the stories based on the headlines alone, and they argued that such things serve as further proof that Trump is too dishonest to be a good president.

Having our personal biases and preferences shape our perception of reality is not good, but as Christians, it is even worse when we let our biases and preferences shape our points of view on Christianity and the Bible. We need to be better than this today.

Are we guilty of having our passions dictate how we interpret God's Word? Do our views shape our understanding of the Bible, or does the Bible shape our understanding of who we are called to be and how we are called to act? We should meditate on this truth today.

Day 42

John Quincy Adams

1 Thessalonians 5:22 "Stay away from every kind of evil."

Henry Clay was born on April 12, 1777, and I needed a date that I could somehow shoehorn into today's devotion, so here we are.

In the Election of 1824, Clay used his influence as Speaker of the House to make John Quincy Adams the President of the United States. The election had several good candidates to choose from, so no one got a majority of electoral votes, throwing the decision into the House of Representatives where Clay wielded his power. After Adams secured his victory, he named Clay as his secretary of state.

This was more than just a political favor for Clay. With the election of Adams to the White House, it now meant that America had had four presidents in a row who had earlier served as secretary of state. This position was seen as the stepping stone to the presidency.

It looked as if Clay and Adams had made a deal. People back then imagined Adams saying to Clay, "If you make me the sixth president, I'll set you up to be the seventh." Supporters of Andrew Jackson called it a "corrupt bargain," and the term has lived on in history class lectures for almost two hundred years.

Adams did not break the law, but it did look like a dirty, smarmy thing that someone might do if he was a totally self-serving politician. Adams should have avoided the appearance of evil.

Are we vulnerable to making the kind of mistake Adams made? Do we get so focused on achieving a worthy goal that we become oblivious to how our actions might be perceived? It is easy to forget that we should strive for more than just the right results; we need to do things the right way. Do we need to avoid the appearance of evil in the things we are involved in today?

Day 43

Ulysses Grant

Romans 12:18 "If possible, as far as it depends on you, live at peace with everyone."

Ulysses Grant and his wife both demonstrated this virtue, and it saved the life of the future president. Julia Grant did not like Mary Todd Lincoln. Perhaps Mrs. Grant did not like Mary Lincoln's jealous nature, or maybe it was the First Lady's materialism, vanity, occasional weirdness, or some unholy combination thereof.

In her defense, the First Lady could be charming, she was a nice dresser, and she was smart, but those other characteristics were too much for Julia Grant to put up with.

Rather than be miserable in Mary Lincoln's company, Mrs. Grant refused the invitation to go to the theater with the Lincolns on April 14, 1865. Julia wanted a peaceful evening, and Ulysses valued maintaining the peace with his wife more than he valued an evening with the First Family, so he agreed to Julia's decision.

The same hatred that drove John Wilkes Booth to kill Abe Lincoln would have compelled the assassin to kill Grant, too. But the Grants were not in Ford's Theater that night, allowing Grant to live on and eventually become the eighteenth president.

There is some definite value in avoiding toxic people. For most of us, the upside won't be as dramatic as it was for the Grants, but it is still good advice. Let us pray for wisdom in our relationships today.

Day 44

Andrew Johnson

Proverbs 18:2 "A fool does not delight in understanding, but only wants to show off his opinions."

It wasn't easy being Andrew Johnson.

He was accused of being drunk on his vice-presidential inaugural day. He was dreadfully sick with the flu (allegedly) and had decided not to appear in public, but that just wouldn't do. Abraham Lincoln had been president for four years with Hannibal Hamlin as his vice president, but Republican party leaders wanted to send a unifying message to the country, so they made a switch.

Andrew Johnson had been a Democrat, and he was a southerner. He was the only member of Congress from a Rebel state who did not resign as the Civil War approached. All of this made him an attractive running mate for Lincoln, who wanted to bring the country together.

Given his PR value, Johnson could not be sidelined on Inauguration Day in 1864. Feverish and weak, and fortified with some strong drink from an associate, Johnson faced a crowd of spectators and gave a speech. Perhaps it was not the best time for Johnson to tear into the rich and powerful, given that he was speaking to the rich and powerful, but with his mind sufficiently clouded he reacted against a lifetime of hardships and slights.

He made a fool out of himself. If he wasn't drunk that day (and he probably was not), he certainly looked that way. If we're ever so upset that we're tempted to insult a bunch a people, maybe we should stay silent.

Did Johnson learn a lesson that day?

Can we?

Day 45

Harry Truman

Psalm 17:6 "I call on You, God, because You will answer me; listen closely to me; hear what I say."

On April 17, 1952, Harry Truman signed a bill empowering the president to pick one day each year to serve as the National Day of Prayer. Interestingly, according to the legislation, this Day of Prayer could not be on a Sunday.

To a degree, it was a political move. During the 1950s, the United States was experiencing the Cold War with the atheistic Soviet Union, and church attendance across the nation was at a high point, so legislation that was pro-God would play well with the voters back home. But not every politician was a cynic. It makes sense that a nation with many Christian people would see some genuinely Christian politicians bubble up to the surface.

Thus, the motives behind the Day of Prayer are gray. A combination of true believers and opportunists joined together in a common cause.

In the same way, sometimes prayers are offered by sincere people with good theology for the Lord's purposes. But some prayers don't quite meet that standard.

How are we going to pray today? Will we pray for the Lord's agenda or our own? Are we going to have faith that God can answer those prayers, or do we lack faith but figure we have nothing to lose?

Let us pray for the Lord's will and not our own. Let us pray earnestly and frequently today.

Day 46

William McKinley

1 Peter 2:13A "Submit to every human authority because of the Lord."

The United States entered into a short conflict known as the Spanish-American War on April 21, 1898, during the administration of President William McKinley. The media had been clamoring for war much earlier than this for reasons both noble and otherwise. McKinley took some heat for delaying in asking Congress to declare war (which was how we went to war back when we followed the Constitution on this subject, but let's not open that can of worms).

When the battleship *Maine* blew up under suspicious circumstances, McKinley's hand was forced.

Why had McKinley hesitated? Was he weak? Was he a coward? Actually, he had fought in the Civil War, the bloodiest war in US history. Having seen war firsthand, he was not anxious to send other young men off to experience it.

It is easy to get frustrated when those running the show aren't as bold and decisive as we want them to be. Instead of being so quick to be disappointed, we should try to understand their points of view. We need to respect those in authority over us for the reasons I have mentioned, and because Scripture commands it.

Some of us question God when we are frustrated or hurt by how things have turned out. It is not wrong to try and understand things, but our goal needs to be to trust God even when we do not get the answers we seek. There is a difference between asking why and doubting.

On a personal note, questions are important to me, but I have never asked God why my wife died suddenly at age 52. It was the worst loss I have ever suffered, but I believe He is good, so I submit to His will.

We are called to submit to God and our earthly authorities.

Day 47

Abraham Lincoln

1 Peter 5:6-7 "Humble yourselves, therefore, under the mighty hand of God, so that He may exalt you at the proper time, casting all your cares on Him, because He cares about you."

On April 22, 1864, the Civil War was happening. And we were in the midst of election campaigning. Those things were undoubtedly factors in the decision by Congress on this date to put "In God We Trust" on our new coins.

Money periodically has gotten a new look throughout American history. A future president, Theodore Roosevelt, expressed misgivings about putting this message on our currency. He wondered if it sent the message that money was our God.

But back in 1864, Abraham Lincoln, a man who never formally joined a church but increasingly made faith-oriented statements as president, signed Congress' bill.

We put "In God We Trust" on our money, but do we live by this motto today? This devotion is not about America as a whole; it's about us as the Church.

Do we trust God or our money?

Do we trust God or our circumstances?

Do we trust God or the opinions of others?

As believers we say we trust God, but does our thought life communicate a different message? Are we driven by worry? Are most of our decisions fear-based?

Let us repeat to ourselves throughout the day, as we face good news and bad, "I place my trust in God, not my circumstances."

Day 48

Abraham Lincoln

Matthew 17:21 "However, this kind does not come out except by prayer and fasting."

At the height of the Civil War, Abraham Lincoln called for a day of "national humiliation, fasting, and prayer." It was April 30, 1863.

Did it work? Barely more than two months later, the decisive Union victories at Gettysburg and Vicksburg gave the Union the upper hand in the conflict with the Confederacy.

Does God take sides in war? Well, according to the Old Testament, He does, so there's that.

Interestingly, there were plenty of Christians on both sides of the Civil War, and most of them believed that God was definitely on their side.

But the more relevant question for us today is do we believe in humbling ourselves, fasting, and praying? I have heard multiple Christians refer to themselves as "arrogant." While I applaud their self-awareness, I am troubled that when I hear such sentiments it is almost always in a descriptive but not penitent way. The men (I've only heard men say this) do not seem overly bothered by their arrogance. The Bible clearly calls us to humility, not self-pride.

That said, I struggle with fasting. I've fasted twice. Once I ate a late breakfast and an early supper, but I skipped lunch, and as they (used to) say the struggle was real. The other time I fasted, it was for a medical procedure, and the less said about that, the better. Suffice it to say, I have not fasted regularly.

Many Christians struggle with prayer. It's not that we don't believe in it. We just don't always do it.

Humility, fasting, and prayer—which of these areas do we need to surrender to the Lord? We all have room for spiritual growth, so what are we going to do about it today?

Day 49

Dwight Eisenhower

Acts 13:1-2 "Now in the church at Antioch there were prophets and teachers: Barnabas, Simeon who was called Niger, Lucius of Cyrene, Manaen, a close friend of Herod the tetrarch, and Saul. As they were worshipping the Lord and fasting, the Holy Spirit said, 'Set apart for me Barnabas and Saul for the work to which I have called them.'"

May 8, 1945 marked the end of World War Two in Europe. The surrender of Germany meant that Dwight "Ike" Eisenhower's huge project was over. He had served as Supreme Commander of Allied Forces in the Western Theater of the war. This meant, among other things, that he had planned the North Africa campaign and the biggest invasion of all time at Normandy, France.

Eisenhower was 54 years old, so he was really too young to retire. But imagine being in his shoes. What could one do for an encore after helping win World War Two? It might be hard to find a career path that could hold one's interest after that.

Ultimately, Ike served eight years as President of the United States. He guided America through a tumultuous time during the Cold War, and he maintained his popularity with the American people. In short, he found work that was comparable in scope to his last job—it was sufficient to keep his interest.

Transitions can be tricky in our spiritual lives, too. After a mountaintop experience, it is easy to get a little lost trying to figure out what's next. Sometimes we want to hold onto an old memory instead of making a new one, as if one close encounter with God is supposed to tide us over throughout this life.

Paul (then called Saul) was successfully working in a church when God called him to start his great missionary journeys. Let us look for what God has for us next. Let's assume there is a next until God calls us home.

Day 50

John Adams

Ephesians 3:20-21 "Now to Him who is able to do above and beyond all that we ask or think according to the power that works in us—to Him be glory in the church and in Christ Jesus to all generations, forever and ever. Amen."

On May 9 1798, President John Adams called for a day of fasting and prayer. Times were tense with France and Great Britain. Both countries were intercepting our ships and confiscating our goods in an effort to disrupt each other's economies. We were a poor country and not equipped to fight either power, though we did build up our navy and then fought the French in the Atlantic in what is often referred to by historians as the Quasi War.

Adams was not an orthodox Christian, because he did not believe in the deity of Christ, or that Christ died for our sins. But Adams did believe in a loving Creator God who cared for those who served Him. Thus, it is not surprising that Adams knew America needed more than a decent navy if we were going to survive. This led to his appeal for fasting and prayer.

Just recently, there was a devotion dedicated to humility, fasting, and prayer. If you think you have maxed out your potential in these areas, you can go ahead and skip to the next reading.

As I was working on this devotion, I got a card in the mail from my friends Jeff and Sheri Stewardson. The card had the perfect Scripture for today. God calls us to communicate with Him, and He is capable of doing much more than we can imagine asking for, so why wouldn't we reach out to Him today and ask for His mercy and guidance? He is more than great, and He loves us. May we pray with confidence today.

Day 51

Zachary Taylor

Proverbs 25:11 "A word spoken at the right time is like gold apples in silver settings."

On May 15, 1842, General Zachary Taylor began a couple of days of serious negotiations with several Native American tribes. They did not talk about easy things. For example, Taylor told these tribes to stay out of Texas, which was provocative, to say the least. But he wasn't bullying these tribes—he promised to pay ransoms for white children who had been kidnapped. He made a big demand, and he made a big offer.

Serious progress was made.

It is interesting what can be accomplished when we are willing to open up and then keep communicating. Too often, we are unwilling to deal with big problems. When we are mad or hurt, it is easier to talk about someone than it is to talk to him or her. For some of us, it is easier to be passive-aggressive than it is to just be honest. Others of us get frustrated that the other person doesn't just somehow telepathically know what we are thinking and feeling.

When we have a problem, we need to at least try and talk it out. Who knows? Maybe the other person is just as hurt about something as we are. Maybe we are as oblivious to the pain we caused them as they are oblivious to the pain they caused us.

Whether we're sharing our hurt or trying to fix a problem, talking it out, while challenging, can make all the difference in the world.

Day 52

William Howard Taft

Acts 9:5-6 "'Who are you, Lord?' Saul said. 'I am Jesus, the One you are persecuting,' He replied. 'But get up and go into the city, and you will be told what you must do.'"

Yale's graduation day in 2019 was May 19. William Howard Taft actually graduated in 1878, but do you know how hard it is to figure out when Yale's graduation took place in 1878? Wait, I'll save you the trouble of guessing—it's really hard.

Taft finished second in his class. He looked like he was destined for greatness, and he attained that, but his presidency was kind of a disaster.

Sometimes people seem like they will be totally successful, but they fail.

Sometimes people look like they won't amount to much, but they do. We need to stop making ironclad assumptions based solely on circumstances.

We are shaped by our experiences. But as believers, we are new creations in Christ, and we have the power of the Holy Spirit working through us. If God is for us, who can be against us?

Seriously. If God is for us who can be against us? We don't have to end the journey where we started it. Just look at the example of Saul/Paul. He went from persecuting Christians to writing half the books in the New Testament.

Let us live like we believe that today we are not defined by the successes or failures of yesterday. Let us be defined by the King we serve.

Day 53

George Washington

Acts 15:39-40 "They had such a sharp disagreement that they parted company, and Barnabas took Mark with him and sailed off to Cyprus. But Paul chose Silas and departed, after being commended by the brothers and sisters to the grace of the Lord."

On May 28, 1754, a 22-year-old George Washington led a small force of Virginians, and he—along with some Native American allies—confronted a party of French soldiers and a diplomat (or a spy, depending on who you ask). Tensions were high. It wouldn't be long before the French and Indian War was going to start.

On this particular morning, shots were fired. The French were quickly beaten, and then they got slaughtered. The French blamed Washington; Washington blamed the Native Americans.

What's the takeaway for today? One could actually go in two directions. It's either (1) if you are going to be a leader, people will say bad things about you, or (2) even great people make mistakes.

When we try to do the right thing, it's hard. If great leaders like Paul, Barnabas, and George Washington struggle to make right decisions, it stands to reason that we will struggle too on occasion. It's tough to do the right thing because we are sinners, and we are surrounded by sinners. There are days when our choices are black and white, and there are other days when all of our options seem gray. But failing to make decisions? That doesn't always work either. What can we do? We can lean on the Lord for guidance today. Let's lean on Him for big decisions and little ones, too.

Day 54

Andrew Jackson

Psalm 29:3 "The voice of the Lord is above the waters. The God of glory thunders—the Lord, above the vast waters…"

As Andrew Jackson was talking to someone on May 29, 1845, the former president said, "Sir, I am in the hands of a merciful God. I have full confidence in His goodness and mercy…The Bible is true."

Psalm 29 speaks of the thunderous power of God. Jackson spoke of the mercy of God. Both qualities make the other more impressive.

Ten days later, the seventh President of the United States passed away. Jackson put his faith in a merciful God and His Word. Did the former president go to Heaven? We will never know, this side of Glory. What Jackson said is somewhat short of the explicit recognition of belief in Jesus as Savior and Lord, but we only know what the records tell us. We do not know everything Jackson said or thought regarding Jesus.

But the question today is not what Jackson meant when he said he believed the Bible; it's what we mean when we say we believe it. Do we believe the Bible to the point that we live by its commands, or do we only believe the Bible when it is convenient? The Bible says to forgive, but some people really hurt us. The Bible says for us to be people of integrity, but everyone knows you've got to go along to get along at work.

Do we believe that the God of glory is up in Heaven thundering? Do we trust His power to protect us when life seems too hard? Do we trust His mercy? Let us pray today that the Holy Spirit would help us put our trust in Him.

Day 55

Calvin Coolidge

Romans 13:8 "Do not owe anyone anything, except to love one another, for the one who loves another has fulfilled the law."

June 2, 1924, was the day Calvin Coolidge signed the Indian Citizenship Act, which officially recognized Native Americans as US citizens.

Later, a photo was taken of Coolidge wearing a Native American headdress. One might say he looked ridiculous, especially since he was wearing a three-piece suit.

It might be easy for someone to think Coolidge was mocking a minority. In an age where politicians are hounded for racially insensitive choices made years earlier (like white politicians wearing blackface and thinking it was funny), it would be easy to see Coolidge's picture and think the worst.

Actually, it was part of a ceremony where he was adopted by a tribe of Sioux. Coolidge was being honored by Native Americans, and he was appreciative of it.

Nevertheless, sometimes the racism is real, even in the twenty-first century. What do we do as Christians? Are we partially responsible for it? Are we so quick and passionate in complaining about false accusations that it leaves us blind to real instances of racism? Rather than laughing along with someone's insensitive remark, what if we just…didn't? What if we asked people how they feel instead of explaining how we think they should feel?

People are supposed to know we are Christians by our love, but some believers disrespect other races. If we're guilty of that, we need to repent. If we see our brothers and sisters commit this sin, we need to lovingly confront them.

Day 56

Ronald Reagan

Jeremiah 29:11 "For I know the plans I have for you."

On June 7, 1982, Ronald Reagan met with Pope John Paul II. The two men had a unique and rather horrifying thing in common: Both survived assassination attempts. It made sense that John Paul, as head of the Catholic Church, would find a spiritual meaning in the experience, but Reagan did, too. They bonded over the shared feeling that God had a special plan for their lives, because they had been spared when death was close at hand.

Do we feel that God has a special plan for our lives? Maybe we need to be reminded of that because life has hit us hard. Perhaps some of us are feeling kind of worthless or neglected by God these days, because our plans never seem to work out. There are those of us who look at the gifts, talents, and opportunities others have, and we feel pretty insignificant in comparison.

But what if we weren't supposed to be comparing ourselves in that way at all?

The upside in comparing ourselves to others is we can learn and grow. God never intended for comparisons to grind us down (though sometimes learning from others allows for sin to be grounded out of our lives).

No one is insignificant. God has a special plan for us to serve and glorify Him on this day and for the rest of our days.

Day 57

Andrew Jackson

1 Peter 1:15-16 "But as the One who called you is holy, you also are to be holy in all your conduct; for it is written, 'Be holy because I am holy.'"

Andrew Jackson died of congestive heart failure. A contributing factor was lead poisoning from two bullets that had been lodged inside him for years, mementos of his dueling ways. On June 12, 1845, his funeral sermon was interrupted by Jackson's parrot, which started cussing so loudly that it had to be removed from the room.

If one wanted to get really specific about the moral of the story, it would be don't teach a parrot how to cuss. But we can step back from that and come up with a broader principle.

Sometimes people engage in behaviors that they know are probably not good (we could refer to such activities as "sin"). It might be something that seems victimless or innocuous (like, I don't know, teaching a parrot how to swear). It might be behavior that we think is no one else's business or we think no one will find out about.

The unfortunate thing about sin, though, is once we start down that path, we can't always control it. And we don't know what we can't control until, well, we've lost control. We don't always know what the consequences of such behavior will be. And we don't know who might find out about it or when.

All of the above are fine reasons for us to make good decisions, but there is an even better one: Sin in our lives is a barrier we put up between ourselves and the God who loves us.

Teaching a parrot to swear is just silly in the overall scheme of things, but the topic of the day is not. It is God's will that we strive for holiness—for blameless behavior before Him. Let's do that today.

Day 58

George HW Bush

Colossians 3:14 "Above all, put on love, which is the perfect bond of unity."

On June 12, 2014, George HW Bush celebrated his 90th birthday by jumping out of an airplane.* He was a World War Two fighter pilot, so he had some experience with airplanes and the jumping out thereof. And he had also celebrated his last few milestone birthdays (75, 80, and 85) in the same fashion.

On this day in 1942, Bush joined the Navy. He was 18, and he chose to delay going to college so he could risk his life serving his country. For a while, he was the youngest fighter pilot in the Navy. Bush was a legitimate war hero, but people did not hear a whole lot about that when Bush ran for president.

Do we *really* know the people around us, or are we so caught up in our circumstances that we are oblivious to the battles they have fought (militarily in the case of Bush and metaphorically in the case of many of us)?

We need to care about people. Maybe today is the day that some of us busy people stop and get to know someone in our orbit. We can show the love the Bible tells us to display by taking an interest in someone and learning that person's story. This might be the day we learn the name of a person who works with us, someone we haven't paid much attention to before.

Let's care about somebody enough to learn something about him/her today. Such an act of love would be a great way to plant a seed for Christ.

*He wore a parachute. I just wanted you to know that in case you were thinking of celebrating your birthday similarly.

Day 59

James Polk

James 1:5 "Now if any of you lacks wisdom, he should ask God—who gives to all generously and ungrudgingly—and it will be given to him."

James Polk was a workaholic. He never slowed down. He died on June 15, 1849, when he was only 53. And if those were all the facts I gave you, you might draw the conclusion that he must have died as a result of working too hard.

In reality, he died of cholera, which is not caused by overwork. There was no connection between the two.

We need to avoid the temptation to jump to conclusions.

It is all too easy to base assumptions on this cool Latin phrase, *post hoc ergo propter hoc*. It means "after this, therefore because of this."

We jump to conclusions about situations, and we assume we know more than we do. We stress and fret over things. We see possibilities and we assume disaster is coming.

We notice A + B and tell people that C has happened. Sometimes C doesn't happen, and then we're embarrassed.

We see someone who is unhappy, and we wonder why they are mad at us. Maybe he/she is just having a bad day.

We beat ourselves up. Some of us say we are sorry for things we should not apologize for. We all know people like that. Something is wrong, and they assume somehow it is their fault for either causing it or not figuring out how to fix it.

Today might be a day when we start to slow ourselves down. Let us pray for the wisdom to not overreact and jump to conclusions.

Day 60

Zachary Taylor

Colossians 3:15 "And let the peace of Christ, to which you were also called in one body, rule your hearts. And be thankful."

On June 17, 1835, Zachary Taylor's daughter, Sarah Knox Taylor, married Jefferson Davis. Zachary Taylor was not yet president. Jefferson Davis would later become the one and only president of the Confederate States of America, in addition to being in Franklin Pierce's Cabinet as secretary of war (a post that was later renamed secretary of defense).

Today, we're looking at President Zachary Taylor, and the old saying, "You can pick your friends, but you can't pick your family."

Jefferson Davis was the son-in-law of a man who would later become president. Taylor and his daughter both died before the birth of the Confederacy, which is probably for the best. Those extended family dinners during Thanksgiving would have been pretty awkward.

The point is family dynamics can be tough. Biological, adoptive, in-laws—it can all get challenging. Over the years, we've been around for all the bad ideas and big mistakes of our relatives and vice versa. We know their flaws, and they know ours.

Family members can be awesome, and they can also be a challenge.

Let's pray today for an extra measure of grace for that difficult family member.

Day 61

Theodore Roosevelt

2 Timothy 2:15 "Be diligent to present yourself to God as one approved, a worker who doesn't need to be ashamed, correctly teaching the word of truth."

The War of 1812 began on June 18 of that year. Theodore Roosevelt later wrote a book on this conflict, entitled *The Naval War*, when he was a member of the New York State Assembly.

Roosevelt would go on to become the assistant secretary of the Navy, a US Army colonel during the Spanish-American War, and, of course, President of the United States.

This man who would be involved in the navy, and war, and overseeing our foreign policy had spent much time studying such things.

What are we doing to prepare ourselves to spend the rest of our lives as Christian disciples? Most of us could not write a book on the Bible or discipleship, and that is okay. God did not call everyone to be a writer, and frankly, I'm glad. I couldn't handle all the competition.

That said, we do need to be studying what it means to be a disciple. Maybe that does mean writing a book, or at least reading one, or going on a mission trip, or…anything that would help us grow in our faith. God has wired us differently from one another for a reason, so it is okay that we do not all learn the same way. But we need to figure out, prayerfully, how to grow in our faith.

Day 62

James Monroe

Proverbs 11:2 "When arrogance comes, disgrace follows, but with humility comes wisdom."

On June 21, 1788, the Constitution became official when the ninth state out of thirteen ratified it. With this decision by the New Hampshire state legislature, the Constitution would be the law of the land.

James Monroe opposed it. He had been a hero in the American Revolution against tyranny, and he hated the idea of giving too much power to this new government. He was afraid American government officials could become tyrants as easily as British officials had.

Fortunately, Monroe quickly made his peace with the idea of the new government. He became an ambassador under his hero George Washington and again under Thomas Jefferson. Monroe held two Cabinet positions in the James Madison administration before he became president himself for two terms.

Imagine if Monroe had been stubborn and unyielding. Imagine if Monroe had been embarrassed at being on the losing side of the constitutional debate and couldn't get past it. The USA could have lost out on a successful politician and a popular president. (When Monroe ran for re-election as president, he received every electoral vote but one. That isn't bad.)

Monroe was willing to change his mind on a big issue without being self-conscious about it. He did not let his promising political career get derailed by pride.

Pride can kill our Christian witness. Pride is totally the opposite of the attitude we have been called to display. Someone reading this needs to repent of the sin of pride today.

Day 63

Abraham Lincoln

Philippians 4:7 "And the peace of God, which surpasses all understanding, will guard your hearts and minds in Christ Jesus."

In 1836, a man named Robert Allen said he had information that would, if he chose to release it, ruin the career of young Abraham Lincoln. On June 21 of that year, Lincoln wrote a letter to the man that was both direct and funny. The future sixteenth president told Mr. Allen that it was flattering that Allen was so thoughtful as to not share Lincoln's secret. Lincoln was grateful for such a favor because, he said, "No one has needed more favors than I, and, generally, few have been less unwilling to accept them." But Lincoln goes on to say he must decline the favor; Allen should tell his secret.

Lincoln then was gracious enough to say that whatever this secret is, and Lincoln says he has no idea what it might be, he trusts that Allen believed it was true.

There is so much we can learn from Lincoln's approach to this attempt at character assassination. Lincoln confronted the man directly. Lincoln's humor showed that he was not worried or stressed out about what people might think—he was cool under pressure. And he managed to say he was innocent of wrongdoing without calling the man a liar.

It's tough to keep our cool when people try to get a rise out of us. Do we act, or do we react? Ultimately, we can't control other people. We can't even control ourselves all the time, but with God's help we can have a peace that passes understanding. That's the gift that can give us grace under pressure today.

Day 64

James Buchanan

1 Thessalonians 5:11 "Therefore encourage one another and build each other up as you are already doing."

Siam became Thailand on June 23, 1939. It flip-flopped between Siam and Thailand later on, but that's not the point here. Back when it was still Siam, more specifically during the administration of the fifteenth President of the United States, James Buchanan, the King of Siam gave Buchanan a herd of elephants.

Of course, this begs the question, "What in the world was Buchanan supposed to do with a herd of elephants?"

There are times in life when we, like the King of Siam, want to give something that is easy for us to hand out, but the person on the receiving end doesn't want it or need it. The "gift" we might be so quick to give could be judgment, condemnation, or unsolicited advice. What if instead we gave extravagantly of our time, compassion, and encouragement?

Encouragement—genuine and specific encouragement—does not cost us anything, but it can be life-changing for the recipient.

Don't we want to have a life-changing impact?

Aren't we called to have a life-changing impact?

Let us pray for wisdom regarding who we can encourage today.

Day 65

Franklin Pierce

Colossians 1:11 "...being strengthened with all power, according to his glorious might, so that you may have great endurance and patience..."

The General Court in Boston approved a charter for a small college called Bowdoin on June 24, 1795. Twenty-nine years later, Franklin Pierce graduated third in his class.

What makes Pierce's accomplishment pretty impressive is the fact that he had sunk to last in his class during his sophomore year.

What makes his achievement look a little less impressive is the fact that there were only fourteen students in his graduating class.

Still, moving from last place to third is significant.

What about us? How do we respond to setbacks? How are we responding to a current situation that hasn't been working out for us? Do we give up? Do we feel sorry for ourselves?

Some doors are just not going to open for us, no matter how badly we want what is on the other side. But maybe, instead of assuming that every closed door is a locked door, we need to approach the issue differently. We should pray for wisdom, focus, and/or endurance. A trendy term for endurance these days is "grit." Perhaps today is the day to try again—to show some grit.

Obviously, this could have applications to several areas of our lives, including work and relationships, but what about spiritually? Is there an area of ministry we need to embrace, or are there people in our lives to whom we need to be a witness? Have we just about given up? Maybe instead we should show some grit, and if we are convinced that we don't have any left, let's pray to the One who gives abundantly, so that we may do His will despite our discouragement.

Day 66

Ulysses Grant

Proverbs 27:17 "Iron sharpens iron, and one person sharpens another."

On June 24, 2019, I engaged in a futile search to verify the date of an event. The matter at hand occurred in the life of Ulysses Grant while he was serving as the eighteenth President of the United States. Grant got ticketed and fined for speeding. What makes this especially remarkable is that Grant lived and died before people drove cars.

The president was speeding in a horse and carriage.

Instead of responding with threats or outrage, Grant complimented the police officer who gave him the ticket. The president respected the man's conscientious commitment to duty.

Grant went on to pay his $20 fine without a fuss.

And how about us? Are we penitent when we are caught doing wrong, or do we get defensive? Do we make justifications? Do we tell people that whatever we do is none of their business?

As a Christian, I am part of a body, and what happens to one part of the body can impact the rest of it. As a Christian, I am part of a family that is supposed to care about me and want what is best for me. That has to include the right for members of the family to speak up when it is for my benefit.

None of us are perfect. We all benefit from accountability. At times we need to be receptive to it, and at times we need to be willing to speak up and offer it. Let's pray to have grace in both scenarios.

Day 67

Andrew Johnson

1 Corinthians 6:14 "God raised up the Lord and will also raise us up by His power."

On June 25, 1824, a guy named James Selby offered a $10 reward for anyone who would return his no-good, ungrateful apprentices, one of whom was Andrew Johnson.

Johnson's family was so poor, they sold their son out to go work for Selby. It wasn't exactly slavery, but it wasn't totally different. Young Johnson was not free to go and get another job until the terms of the contract signed by his parents had expired.

Andrew Johnson was so miserable, however, that he ran away from Selby, even though this was against the law.

The uneducated apprentice Andrew Johnson went from these humble origins to the most powerful office in the country. If Johnson could rise to such heights, what might we, empowered by the Holy Spirit, accomplish for the Kingdom of God? What is holding us back, besides a lack of faith?

In a surprise move I will answer my own question. A lack of talent, ambition, and circumstances might also be holding us back. I am willing to guess that Andrew Johnson probably had a lot more pluck than the average person. Yep, Johnson was plucky.

The good news is it is okay if we don't measure up to Andrew Johnson, because God is probably not calling any of us to rise to the presidency.

The even better news is that we still have the power of the Holy Spirit. And, really, if we believe in a miracle-working God, then we need to believe that He is more than sufficient to accomplish whatever thing, great or small, He wants to achieve through us.

Let's pray for the faith that God will use us today.

Day 68

James Garfield, John Kennedy, George W. Bush

Ruth 1:16 "But Ruth replied, 'Don't plead with me to abandon you or to return and not follow you. For wherever you go, I will go, and wherever you live, I will live; your people will be my people, and your God will be my God.'"

On June 26, 1963, John Kennedy famously said "*Ich bin ein Berliner*," which translates to "I am a Berliner." He said this to show his solidarity with West Berlin in a time when that area was under the threat of a takeover by Communist forces during the Cold War. It was an electrifying moment.

This was not the first time a president famously spoke German. James Garfield did it shortly before his presidency. He was addressing German-speaking Americans to win their votes. This would have been something German Americans had never experienced before—a presidential candidate showing them the respect of speaking to them in their native language.

Garfield spoke German. Kennedy spoke German. George W. Bush spoke Spanish to Spanish-speaking Texans.

Language can create a powerful connection. How might we convey such respect to others? How can we reach people at such a level that they know our hearts and our desire that they be saved from their sin? Can we connect with them at such a level that they want what we have? Maybe we need to love them that much.

Day 69

George Washington

Proverbs 10:9 "The one who lives with integrity lives securely, but whoever perverts his ways will be found out."

There was an interesting headline on an Internet video on June 27, 2019. It posed the question of whether or not George Washington ever participated in a debate. This was intriguing because Washington never campaigned for the presidency, and he was elected unanimously by the Electoral College for both of his terms. Presidential debates typically did not happen back then. I had never read of Washington being in a formal debate of any kind, and I could not imagine a scenario whereby he might have been.

Intrigued, I clicked on the video, and it revealed a quick answer: No, he didn't engage in a debate. Then, the person being interviewed took the discussion in a different direction. The title of the video did not convey the content very well at all. Technically, it did answer the question, so there's that. But as a viewer, I did not get what I was expecting.

Do we do falsely advertise in the church?

Do we do that as believers?

Are we guilty of misrepresenting our faith or our church in order to pull people in or get them to give us attention? Are we guilty of skewing truths about ourselves in our interactions with others? Do we compromise the truth to be liked, to fit in, or to get ahead? Let us pray for the courage to be authentic today.

Day 70

George Washington, Woodrow Wilson

Philippians 3:17 "Join in imitating me, brothers and sisters, and pay careful attention to those who live according to the example you have in us."

It was June 27, 2019, when a friend I've known since middle school, Greg Williams, told me something I should have known but didn't: Woodrow Wilson wrote a biography of George Washington.

Washington was a role model for Wilson. It makes sense that a man like Wilson, who aspired to leadership and eventually became the 28th President of the United States, might decide he had something to learn from an intense study of the first president.

Who is your role model?

Mine is a man named Mark Smith. When I met him, his career goal was to be a history professor. But he also really had a passion for preaching, and he did that, too, as often as he got the opportunity. I could relate to that. But there was more. Mark shared with me his love of old movies, and we played chess together. He was a mentor and a friend.

We need role models. We need people from whom we can learn.

We also need to be role models for those who are not as far along on the journey as we are.

Who are we learning from, and who are we helping? We should prayerfully consider those questions today.

Day 71

George Washington

Galatians 6:9 "Let us not get tired of doing good, for we will reap at the proper time if we don't give up."

George Washington's British problem took a turn for the worse on June 28, 1776, when the British came streaming into New York by the thousands. Washington's troops were already inferior to the Redcoats in training and provisions, and now they were hopelessly outnumbered. For several months, Washington got chased around New York. He spent his time alternating between running and getting beaten in battle.

If this were a movie, after a couple of days, Washington would have come up with an amazing plan, or the rest of the Avengers would have shown up and evened the odds, or something. But in real life, things didn't get better right away. The smart money was on the British in 1776…and 1777…and 1778.

It took years for Washington to turn things around. But he did. The British surrender didn't happen until 1781 at Yorktown, but it finally happened.

In our instant gratification society, we want the turnaround to happen fast, or we are tempted to give up.

Maybe that thing hanging over us is truly not a defeat. It might just be a character-building setback. Maybe it's a really rough and drawn-out setback, but it's still a temporary one. Perhaps we need to pray and try again today.

Day 72

Abraham Lincoln

Proverbs 16:18 "Pride comes before destruction, and an arrogant spirit before a fall."

Salmon Chase was the Secretary of the Treasury for Abraham Lincoln. Chase was smart, and he was good at his job, but sometimes his work performance suffered because he was angling to be the next president. At times his ambition got in the way of what was best for his job and the country.

Lincoln needed him, so the sixteenth president tolerated a lot. The stakes were high because the country was torn in half over the Civil War. Lincoln was famously patient with high-ranking government officials and military officers who occasionally crossed the line and communicated disrespect and insubordination. Lincoln was willing to swallow his pride and keep a tight rein on his ego if it served the greater good for his country. Lincoln could tolerate self-serving behavior in others if the good outweighed the bad.

That said, even Abraham Lincoln had his limits.

One day, Chase pushed the president too far, and Lincoln pushed back. Chase offered his letter of resignation, which he had done a few times before. It was a power move—the president needed him and was thus forced to beg Chase to stay. On June 29, 1864, Lincoln changed tactics and accepted the resignation.

Chase was shocked and tried to walk it back, but Lincoln, while patient, was not wishy-washy. He was ready for a change.

We're not indispensable. I would rather you hear that from me before you hear it from your boss, spouse, adult children, or church. We need to do what we do with humility and as an offering to the Lord. Some believers need to pray for humility today.

Day 73

James Garfield

Galatians 6:5 "For each person will have to carry his own load."

On June 30, 1882, Charles Guiteau's sentence of death by hanging was carried out. Guiteau was infamous throughout the country for murdering President James Garfield. Guiteau had argued against the charges on two grounds. One, he said God had taken away his free will during the assassination, so he was not guilty by reason of insanity. He went on to say that he was not mentally insane, but he was legally insane during the crime. Two, he argued, "The doctors killed Garfield. I just shot him."

Given the poor quality of medical care, Guiteau's second argument might have had some merit.

The point is not that Guiteau was crazy, even though he was.

The point is we all might have a little Guiteau in us. What are we guilty of, yet we protest our innocence anyway? Some of us are excellent at not owning our baggage. We point fingers and shift blame like champs.

"Well, I wouldn't have yelled at her, but she got on my nerves, and she knew I was tired."

"I know what I did was wrong, but he started it."

"I shouldn't do what I do, but my dad…"

"I probably went too far there, and I was definitely flirting, but my wife doesn't pay me any attention, and it was nice to be appreciated."

The doctors did what they could to help the president; it wasn't their fault he died. Guiteau's bullet killed him.

We need to take responsibility for our words and actions. This might necessitate some prayers of repentance, but that's okay.

Day 74

Franklin Roosevelt

Isaiah 49:15-16 "Can a woman forget her nursing child, or lack compassion for the child of her womb? Even if these forget, yet I will not forget you. Look, I have inscribed you on the palms of My hands; your walls are continually before Me."

On June 30, 1941, the Franklin D. Roosevelt Library and Museum was opened for business.

At the time, Roosevelt was the most famous man in America—indeed he was one of the most famous men in the world—but he knew he would not always be, so he wanted there to be a record of his impact. He was famous, but someday he might be forgotten. For instance, William McKinley was quite famous at one point. But if you got in a time machine and went back to the year 1900, you could probably walk by McKinley on the street and have no idea who he was.

There is no guarantee that well-known people or things will always stay in people's minds. This begs the question: How can we remember things God has done for us?

Do we keep a record of God's impact? Do we recall His answered prayers? It might be easier to walk by faith if we made an effort to remember what He has done.

Some Christians journal, but many of us don't. One cool practice I read about on social media is to thank God for some blessings as you go to sleep at night. My friend Alyssa Derrington does that—she writes down three things she is thankful for every evening.

By whatever means we do it, we need to recall God's goodness and faithfulness in the midst of our circumstances. It will help us to grow in our faith.

Day 75

Donald Trump

Matthew 15:7-9 "Hypocrites! Isaiah prophesied correctly about you when he said, 'This people honors me with their lips, but their heart is far from me. They worship me in vain, teaching as doctrines human commands.'"

On June 30, 2019, Donald Trump became the first President of the United States to set foot in North Korea. He met there with the North Korean dictator, Kim Jong-un. Some Republicans praised him for this unique accomplishment and wondered what Trump might be able to do on behalf of South Korea and the overarching goal of peace and security in the region. Some Democrats complained that Trump's meeting with the dictator gave the North Korean a legitimacy he did not deserve, and at the same time tarnished the image of the United States.

Both parties made interesting and defensible arguments, but what is more interesting is both parties made the exact opposite arguments during the previous administration when President Obama was open to negotiating with dictators.

Hypocrisy is an ugly thing, and both political parties can be guilty of it.

How about us? Do we Christians let our politics guide our moral arguments about politicians? Do we let our circumstances in our jobs guide our interpretation of how and when to apply Scripture? Do we allow our changing passions to drive our theology? God sees this. Younger believers see it. Nonbelievers see it.

We are prone to weakness. We are sinners. Let us pray for the strength to not be hypocrites today. Let us be consistent in our walk.

Day 76

James Garfield

1 Peter 4:10 "Just as each one has received a gift, use it to serve others, as good stewards of the varied grace of God."

On July 2, 1881, James Garfield was shot. He did not die until September 19 of that same year. He was in bad shape for over two months. He could not perform the functions of his office, but there was nothing in the Constitution about how to handle such a contingency.

We actually didn't have a solution to this until the Twenty-fifth Amendment went into effect in 1967. It said, among other things, that if a president was unable to perform his/her duties, the vice president inherits, perhaps temporarily, all the powers thereof. It has been invoked a few times over the years when a president has had to go under anesthesia.

This was a good amendment. We don't know if a president will have good health for all four years of a term in office. In the same way, we are not guaranteed tomorrow, so we need to prepare ourselves for contingencies. Part of being a good steward of what we have is making a plan for when we won't be able to be a steward of it anymore. Many people, even believers, are uncomfortable thinking about the fact that our time here is limited, but we need to not pretend that we have forever. Let us pray today that we will be good stewards of the gift of the time God has given us.

Day 77

Harry Truman

Ecclesiastes 4:12 "And if someone overpowers one person, two can resist him. A cord of three strands is not easily broken."

1950 was a tough year. The Cold War between the United States, the Soviet Union, and allies on both sides was in full swing. Korea was a land divided between the Communists in the north and the anti-communists in the south. And most Koreans were not particularly happy about this division.

When the North Koreans invaded the south with the intent to take over and impose communism throughout the peninsula, the United Nations decided to do something about it.

The US joined in the operation to liberate South Korea, and Truman debated whether or not to ask Congress to officially declare war. Did Truman have enough authorization, given that the Senate had ratified our membership in the UN? Secretary of State Dean Acheson pointed out that earlier presidents had ordered military operations without congressional approval more than fifty times.

Ultimately, on July 3, 1950, Truman only offered a draft of a resolution of support for Congress to sign. They did not even do that. The problem was that when the war dragged on and the casualty figures began to rise, the popularity of the war declined. Members of Congress, who never officially endorsed the war, thus had a much easier time condemning it and Truman.

Even though we have the power to do something, we should still invite input from others at times, not only so they can help carry the weight of it, but also so we can benefit from their insights.

The Lone Ranger approach is great...in a Lone Ranger movie, but even he had Tonto, and at this point, I am really digressing. The point is there is value in much counsel. We need to remember that today.

Day 78

John Adams

James 4:17 "So it is sin to know the good and yet not do it."

John Adams signed the Alien Enemies Act into law on July 6, 1798. The Alien and Sedition Acts, as they are known when discussed as a group, were passed within a few more days. These laws were discussed in the Day 28 devotion from the point of view of their opponents, Thomas Jefferson and James Madison. As you will recall they were an attack on the First Amendment right of free speech.

The Federalist Party justified the laws, though, on the basis of national survival. The United States was involved in an undeclared naval war with France, known as the "Quasi War," which was previously referenced on Day 50. Federalists argued that in our struggle for survival we did not need people speaking against the government. What the laws did specifically was empower the authorities to arrest newspaper writers who criticized the government. If they were citizens, they could be thrown in jail. If they were foreigners who had not lived here long enough to be citizens, they could be expelled from the country. And the Alien Act increased the number of years a person had to live here before becoming a citizen. This wasn't as random as it sounds; many of our newspaper publishers in this era were foreign-born.

Adams was uncomfortable with the laws, and he was not zealous in the enforcement thereof, but he ended up caught in the middle. Federalists were upset that he did not fully use this mighty hammer he had been given, and Democratic-Republicans were mad that he had signed this unconstitutional set of bills.

We can't compromise with sin. There will be a reckoning. Adams knew he should veto the legislation, but he didn't. What sin are we trying to compromise with today?

Day 79

Richard Nixon

Romans 3:23 "For all have sinned and fall short of the glory of God."

Richard Nixon's troop withdrawals started in Vietnam on July 8, 1969. It took Nixon four years to do what he had promised he could do in one: end the war and bring our people home. We could label Nixon a liar and move on. Or, we could appreciate his tenacity. Certainly both of those labels fit him at one time or another.

There have been several devotions on the importance of us having grit, so let's not go in that direction this time. What about how we are impacted by someone else's grit? If you were in the service in Vietnam, or if you were a loved one back home, would you be happy that Nixon reached an agreement that got the troops out, or would you be mad that it took so much longer than he said it would?

On second thought, let's not deal with hypotheticals.

What do we do when people in our lives today make a promise and don't deliver how and when they said they would? Do we get angry? Do we talk about them behind their backs? Do we decide we can never count on anyone again?

It makes sense that people let us down periodically. Why wouldn't we let each other down occasionally? We let ourselves down sometimes, and we always try to look out for number one. If I am going to fail to reach my expectations regarding what I want to do for me, of course I'm going to drop the ball when it comes to somebody else. I sin and thus fall short of what I want to do for God, so naturally I will let other people down. With all that in mind, we should pray that God will give us some grace today to help us forgive the imperfections of others.

Day 80

John Adams

1 Samuel 16:23 "Whenever the spirit from God came on Saul, David would pick up his lyre and play, and Saul would then be relieved, feel better, and the evil spirit would leave him."

John Adams signed legislation from Congress on July 11, 1798 that called for the creation of the United States Marine Band. It is interesting that the USA did this, given how poor the government was (literally, financially speaking) back then. Congress recognized that music is important for rallying the troops, soothing the wounded, and inspiring civilians. And Adams agreed.

Music can be an important component in how we relate to God. Music can move us emotionally as we worship.

Conversely, music can create arguments, as we grumble over styles. Probably, the God who created all the sounds and musical instruments (including the vocal one) in the universe is not as picky about music styles as I am. Because God is perfect, the imperfections of our musical offerings, including each of my personal favorites, are all too apparent to Him. I'm guessing He looks on our efforts the way parents look on the artwork of their little children—you love the kids and their earnestness, so you don't hold their shortcomings against them. I wonder how many arguments over music in church are solely about the preferences of the members.

I like to sing, but I wonder sometimes if I get more caught up in the sound of my favorite Christian songs than I do in the spiritual truths I could learn. And do I concentrate on the music more than I focus on worshipping God through the music? I wonder.

Let us pray today that we would have the right attitude about music.

Day 81

Thomas Jefferson

Exodus 14:14 "The Lord will fight for you, and you must be quiet."

One man shot another on July 11, 1804. The victim died the next day. Thomas Jefferson knew both men, but he offered no comment on the sad events.

The shooter was Aron Burr, who happened to be Jefferson's vice president. The victim was Alexander Hamilton, the nation's first Secretary of the Treasury and the founder of the Federalist Party.

Many of those who eulogized Hamilton took the opportunity to champion his political philosophy, but Jefferson could not do that because he hated Hamilton's politics. Praising Hamilton's career would have made Jefferson a hypocrite. Condemning Hamilton would have portrayed Jefferson as an insensitive, opportunistic politician.

There are times when silence is the most prudent course. But silence can be tough, especially in the age of social media. Some people cultivate an echo chamber of like-minded folk. Popping off about something and getting a bunch of "likes" for it can be quite gratifying. It can enhance our self-esteem, at least for a moment.

We should be careful to on the one hand do our part, and on the other hand not try to do the Lord's work for Him. Sometimes the Lord fights our battles for us, and our most prudent course of action is to just keep our mouths shut. Today would be a good day to pray for the wisdom to discern which is which.

Day 82

John Quincy Adams

John 14:6 "Jesus told him, 'I am the way, the truth, and the life. No one comes to the Father except through Me.'"

John Quincy Adams was a religious and church-going man, but he was a Unitarian. Adams did not hold the orthodox, traditional Christian position that God the Father, God the Son, and God the Holy Spirit form a monotheistic Trinity.

His wife, Louisa, did not share his views. Writing in her diary on July 12, 1839, she raised an interesting question. If Jesus "is merely mortal, why were the inspired apostles not equally great?" She pointed out that they, too, were filled with the Holy Spirit, they performed miracles, and they were friends of Jesus, so why did they not have equal status?

John Quincy Adams was a brilliant man with a logical mind, but that did not mean his views were infallible. Some of us have adopted views over the years that might be, like the views of John Quincy Adams, something less than biblical. Maybe we have absorbed some cultural or churchy beliefs that are not consistent with orthodox Christianity. Perhaps we have bought into the teaching of a smart or kind person, who is nevertheless theologically unsound. Maybe we have grown comfortable and even smug with our beliefs. Few of us are as intellectually gifted as Adams, but we are cocky about our views anyway. We have to measure our theology against Scripture. Today could be the day to do that. Let us pray that God would show us if we are in error about Him.

Day 83

Harry Truman

1 Peter 4:8 "Above all, maintain a constant love for one another, since love covers a multitude of sins."

On July 14, 1950, a young evangelist named Billy Graham had the rare privilege of meeting with the leader of the free world, President Harry Truman.

After their talk at the White House, the media asked Graham what the two of them had discussed. The ever-polite Graham, raised by his North Carolina family to be a gentleman, was only too happy to help out all those nice reporters who needed material.

Graham was surprised and flattered by the attention.

On the other hand, "flattered" does not describe how the president felt. From Truman's point of view, Graham had betrayed him. Graham had taken the president's valuable time not to provide spiritual guidance, encouragement, or support, but rather to promote Graham's brand (if I may use a twenty-first-century expression).

Graham's blunder was an innocent one. He had not tried to take advantage of his access to the president, but once Graham realized how it looked, he never made that mistake again.

What about us? Do we support people, do we partner with them, or do we use them for our own agendas? We have to make sure we don't look at people as a means to an end. The greatest commandment is all about love, not our efficiency or the successful completion of our own agendas. Let us pray that we treat people with love today.

Day 84

Chester Arthur

Ephesians 3:12 "In Him we have boldness and confident access through faith in Him."

On July 16, 1854, Lizzie Jennings got kicked off a bus. It was basically a big horse-drawn carriage. Jennings was kicked off because the carriage driver was white, and Lizzie was African American. She was on her way to play the organ at her church for a Sunday morning worship service, but that was clearly not of interest to the carriage driver.

Interestingly, in an age when racial discrimination was common, Ms. Jennings was not content to just accept this mistreatment—she sued. Surprisingly, she won her case, and within a few years the horse-drawn bus industry in her city dropped their racist policies because they didn't want to keep getting sued. Most relevantly for this book, Lizzie Jennings' defense attorney was none other than the future twenty-first president, Chester Arthur.

Who knew?

It's a cool story about doing the right thing, even when it is controversial. Are we bold enough to stand up for what is right when there might be consequences? Do we stand up for ethics in the workplace? Do we stand up to the popular ministry leader who is doing or saying things contrary to Scripture? It's easy for heroes in the movies to do the right thing, but in real life we face an uncertain ending with the risk of real consequences.

Let us pray for the boldness and courage to do the right thing today.

Day 85

Barack Obama

James 1:19 "My dear brothers and sisters, understand this: Everyone should be quick to listen, slow to speak, and slow to become angry."

On July 16, 2009, a police officer arrested an African American man, and it became a national story. The man in question was just sitting in his living room, watching TV and minding his own business when the police officer barged in and began making demands. The law-abiding citizen got angry, and then he got arrested.

When President Barack Obama spoke to the nation about this event, he said he did not have all the information, but that did not stop him from saying the "police acted stupidly."

Things looked different from the officer's point of view. He went to the house because a neighbor called in a "breaking and entering" event there. When the officer entered the premises, adrenaline pumping, he found a man doing something that did not logically compute. Then the man was not cooperative, so the cop arrested him.

Obama encouraged the public to not jump to conclusions, but then he jumped to a conclusion. A little chagrined after the full story came out, the president invited the two men over to the White House for a drink and a civil conversation.

How often do we rush to judgment without all the facts? Do we ever try to fix it afterwards? If a story pushes our buttons, maybe reinforces certain perceptions, are we willing to take a breath and wait for more information? May we pray today for the wisdom to hold our tongues for a moment.

Day 86

Thomas Jefferson

1 Peter 2:16 "Submit as free people, not using your freedom as a cover-up for evil, but as God's slaves."

On July 26, 1775, our first national postal system was created, meaning the post office had been alive and well for several years when Thomas Jefferson developed an issue with it in the late 1790s. Jefferson and his good friend James Madison were the leaders of the Democratic-Republican Party (which later became known as simply the Democratic Party). The opposition, the Federalist Party, was favored by the postmaster general in Jefferson's area. Jefferson became concerned (with good reason) that the Federalists were reading his correspondence and might embarrass him with what they discovered.

Jefferson wasn't discussing anything illegal, but for a while, he pretended to be above party politics, even though, as stated above, he was a party leader. Thus, he wanted to be discreet.

Opening Jefferson's correspondence and reading it wasn't fair of the postmaster general (or legal or cool), but Jefferson's response was interesting: He stopped signing his mail. That way, he could deny it was his if anything embarrassing came out. While I respect Jefferson's privacy, I guess, it was interesting that he didn't just stop writing things that would be embarrassing if discovered.

What about us? Would we be embarrassed if people knew the things we were saying and the schemes we were plotting? Do we try to present one image in public while acting differently behind closed doors? It's hard enough to live one life; trying to lead two different lives is not good math for us. Two-faced smugness is not a good look. May we pray that God would reveal to us any hypocrisy in our lives, and let us pray for the strength to turn away from it.

Day 87

James Polk

Psalm 101:2A "I will pay attention to the way of integrity."

James Polk was a slave owner. Because of this I was surprised to learn that during his administration, Liberia gained its independence. It had been an American colony, and it was founded as a place to send freed slaves.

There were European countries that held on to some of their African colonies until after World War Two, but as of July 26, 1847, Liberia was free from outside rule.

It is interesting that Polk would approve of this, because the idea of Africans being able to manage their own affairs undermined one of the main rationales for slavery. Slave owners had argued that Africans were simpletons who needed guidance like little children. It was this kind of thinking that prompted whites of yesteryear to refer to adult African American males as "boys," and this explains why that practice is so offensive to many African Americans today.

The point here, though, is that Polk did the right thing, even though it was not in his self-interest. How many of us could make this call? The temptation is to say this wouldn't be a struggle for us, because we wouldn't own slaves in the first place. But that misses the point. Apply this truth to our circumstances today. Do we have the integrity to support what is right even when it might be inconvenient for us? It is easy to take the moral high ground when it is an issue that does not really impact us, but what about when it does? What if it means changing our style of worship so that it might better reach other people, even though we don't enjoy it? What if it means changing something at work that would be good for our company or coworkers, but it would require us to take on a task we don't like?

Do we have the integrity to fight for an inconvenient truth?

Day 88

Lyndon Johnson

Psalm 119:9 "How can a young man keep his way pure? By keeping Your word."

On July 28, 1965, Lyndon Johnson decided to raise our military commitment to Vietnam to a total of 125,000 men. We had moved well past the point of saying we were only sending military advisors to help the South Vietnamese. This decision meant war.

Slippery slopes are dangerous things.

Johnson probably wished for a do-over after the Vietnam operation went totally sideways. It looked like a good idea at the time. Communists had taken over in North Vietnam slaughtering tens of thousands who were threats, real or imagined, to their ideology and power. We were in the midst of a Cold War with Communism, and we did not want to see it expand. Many politicians in both the Republican and Democratic Parties believed in the Domino Theory: the idea that if one more country fell to the Communists, it would be that much easier for the next, and the next, and the next.

A decade earlier, we had stopped the Communists in North Korea from taking over South Korea, so why couldn't we do it again? Yet, as Johnson and the country would painfully learn, history only repeats itself until it doesn't. Johnson had gotten us into a war he couldn't get us out of.

How many of us are at the top of a slippery slope morally today? What temptation do we try to justify, as it threatens to pull us into a situation that could destroy our Christian witness? Is there a sexual, financial, or career-based decision that will do us harm? We need to pray for the strength to turn away and go in the other direction.

Don't rationalize a "maybe" where God's Word has clearly said "no."

Day 89

James Buchanan

Psalm 86:5 "For You, Lord are kind and ready to forgive, abounding in faithful love to all who call on You."

Have you ever gotten really down on yourself? Have you felt like a failure? James Buchanan might have been able to relate. As discussed elsewhere, he was an unpopular and unsuccessful president. He messed up a lot.

But it could have been worse.

There was a Russian leader in the 1600s who was so unpopular that a mob beat him to death before setting his remains on fire. Next, they poured his ashes into a cannon and then blew them across a field.

Compared to that guy, James Buchanan was the flavor of the month.

One could argue that his presidency was not a total disaster. Okay, the South did secede from the Union during his single term in office, but I never said Buchanan wasn't a disaster; I said he wasn't a *total* disaster.

Anyway, on July 29, 1858, Japan signed a treaty with the United States, promoting trade and friendship between our two nations. Historically, Japan had wanted nothing to do with outsiders, so this agreement was a pretty big deal for Americans. It was a pretty big deal for Buchanan.

When it comes to how we assess ourselves, a lot of us go through peaks and valleys. We hit points where we struggle to believe in ourselves. Compared to Buchanan, we probably don't look too bad—compared to that Russian guy, we look terrific—but how do we look through God's eyes? We look totally lovable. He loved us so much, He sent Jesus to die for us. Let's find our confidence in God's love today.

Day 90

William Howard Taft

1 Corinthians 6:19-20 "Don't you know that your body is a temple of the Holy Spirit who is in you, whom you have from God? You are not your own, for you were bought at a price. So glorify God with your body."

Sadly, William Howard Taft is most well-known for getting stuck in the White House bathtub. The second thing he is well-known for is…nope, the bathtub thing is pretty much it.

This is not to say that Taft did not accomplish anything else; it's just that the bathtub incident overshadows it all. If people know anything about Taft, it's about the bathtub.

There actually was another interesting thing about Taft and how he interacted with his environment though: He fell asleep a lot. He would drift off in all kinds of situations—after dinner, during conversations, and once during a parade where he was the main event.

I was fascinated to learn this on July 30, 2019.

Taft was an overweight stress eater with an energy level that was too low for his own good.

We should learn from Taft's struggles. We need to take care of ourselves by eating right, exercising, and getting enough sleep.

Strangely, there are two ways we can worship our bodies, and they contradict each other. We can worship our bodies by spending too much time obsessing over our appearance, sacrificing other things in an effort to lose two more pounds or buy the trendiest outfit. But we can also worship our bodies in the opposite way and indulge every craving and impulse that strikes us, whether it originates in our stomachs, our eyes, or wherever.

We need to pray for the strength to not be a slave to our bodies. Our bodies are temples through which we worship God, and as such we should not make them our object of worship.

Day 91

Warren Harding

Judges 6:15 "He (Gideon) said, 'Please, Lord, how can I deliver Israel? Look, my family is the weakest in Manasseh, and I am the youngest in my father's family.'"

Henry Ford was born on July 30, 1863. This is only relevant because he was a significant figure in the early days of the mass production of automobiles. But today's devotion is about President Warren Harding, not Ford.

What does Harding have to do with cars? He was the first president to drive one. Earlier presidents had ridden in cars, but Harding was the first one to get behind the wheel and make something happen. None of the previous twenty-eight presidents had driven a car, but Harding did.

There is nothing particularly special or impressive about Harding compared to our other presidents, and yet he did something that none of his predecessors accomplished.

Is there a lesson in this? I really hope so, since I am devoting our ninety-first devotion to it.

What if you have compared yourself to those around you, and you don't see anything remarkable in you? What if God is going to have you do something unique anyway, even though you don't see yourself as a candidate for such an honor? What if God is choosing you specifically because you do not stand out? I don't know what God has planned for you today (or this week or this month). My point is that it could be something totally unexpected, so we should not sell ourselves short. Though we don't know what His calling might be today, we would do well to pray and to brace ourselves for His service.

91

Day 92

Andrew Johnson

Philippians 3:12 "Not that I have already reached the goal or am already perfect, but I make every effort to take hold of it because I also have been taken hold of by Christ Jesus."

July 31, 1875 is the day Andrew Johnson died. His final job had not come to him easily. He had won a spot in the US Senate in the November 1874 elections, but the seat was so hotly contested that the matter wasn't resolved until January 1875.

Johnson had an up-and-down career to say the least. Just some of the highlights included an earlier stint in the US Senate, a military governorship of Tennessee during the Civil War, the vice presidency, and then the presidency after Lincoln was assassinated. Johnson was impeached by the House of Representatives basically over differing views on Reconstruction in the South after the Civil War. Johnson only survived in office because the Senate came one vote short of the necessary two-thirds majority required to remove him.

After that humiliation, he was re-elected to the Senate a few years later in 1874, but only after the Tennessee legislature voted fifty-six times to make their choice (state legislatures picked US senators back then).

Johnson had soared, then crashed, then soared again. Who would have thought after the humiliation of his impeachment that he would regain such heights? Who would have thought he would be chosen by political leaders in his state after siding with the occupying Union Army? But Johnson persevered, and he went out on top.

The message is clear: Don't quit before the race is over. Sometimes things look bleak, but we don't always know what God has in store for us. We need to press on, continue to reach toward the goal, and finish the race.

Day 93

Warren Harding

Psalm 37:4 "Take delight in the Lord, and He will give you your heart's desire."

On August 2, 1923, Warren Harding's presidency was cut short when he died from a heart attack. He did not lead us to victory during war, nor did he stir the nation with inspiring speeches, but he was the first president to visit Alaska, so there's that.

In the overall scheme of things, it really doesn't matter who the first president was who went to Alaska. That's not much of a legacy. In fairness to Harding, it's not like he bragged about it. But still, as we consider the things we do, it's worth asking this question: What milestones do we want to accomplish in this life?

How much time do we spend chasing goals that won't really matter in the long run? There is nothing wrong with goals themselves, of course. They help us get things done. One of the best ways to accomplish something significant is to set a lot of little and achievable goals along the way. But does something significant wait at the end of the line of all those little goals?

Sometimes it is hard to answer that question by just looking at the big goal itself. There's nothing wrong with setting a goal to make a certain amount of money, for example. The real question is, "What do we want the money for?" Do we want it so we're in a position to help people, impress them, or buy a lot of stuff?

What goals are we striving for? Are they worthy of servants of the Lord? Let's ask the Lord to show us today what He would have us pursue. Instead of asking Him to bless our agenda, may we, as the Psalmist says, "take delight" in Him and His agenda.

Day 94

Benjamin Harrison

Matthew 26:41 "Stay awake and pray, so that you won't enter into temptation. The spirit is willing, but the flesh is weak."

On August 2, 2019, I was traveling in Kentucky when I stopped at a Lee's Famous Recipe restaurant for lunch. Since I was going to be eating alone, I had a book with me. I walked in and left it on a table as I went to the restroom. I was a little concerned about someone taking my book, but I figured it would be okay because I would only be gone a moment, and it was a biography of Benjamin Harrison.

Much to my surprise, when I came out of the bathroom a guy was sitting at my table with my book lying there in front of him. What made this even weirder was there were several empty tables all around him.

If I were awesome, I would have said, "Hey, I have a book just like that."

Instead, I just walked by, scooped up my book, and kept going. The dude never even looked up at me.

I tell this story because it was funny to me. But also it illustrates this point: Sometimes we are where we shouldn't be, like the guy who was sitting with my book. Usually, the consequences are potentially more serious. I mean, I wasn't going to fight the guy over a Benjamin Harrison biography, so the stakes were low. It's not like it was a book on George Washington or something.

Anyway, we need to remove ourselves from certain situations. This guy was at my table, and that was no big deal, but sometimes when we are where we don't belong, the ramifications are life-changing. We need to not dabble with temptation.

Day 95

Ronald Reagan

Hebrews 12:14 "Pursue peace with everyone, and holiness—without it no one will see the Lord."

On August 5, 1981, Ronald Reagan fired 11,500 air traffic controllers who had gone on strike. This was kind of a big deal, since, you know, air traffic controllers help planes land.

Here's the story in a nutshell: The union wanted $10,000 raises for all the air traffic controllers and a reduction in work hours from forty a week to thirty-two. The counteroffer would have added up to $40 million, which sounds like a lot until you consider that what the union asked for would have totaled $770 million. The union decided to call for a strike, even though as federal employees the ATCs were subject to a law that restricted this. President Reagan ordered them not to strike, but they did it anyway. They thought it would be impossible for the airports to operate without them, which would force federal negotiators to give them what they demanded, or at least make a better counteroffer. But it didn't work. The planes kept flying, as air traffic was controlled by supervisors, non-strikers, and some military air traffic controllers.

The striking air traffic controllers weren't as important as they thought they were. They thought they could break the law. They thought if enough of them did it, it would be okay.

People have the same attitude about certain behaviors today. As if it's not really a sin anymore, if enough people are okay with it. Let us pray today that God would help us pursue holiness. We can't break God's laws without consequences.

Day 96

Lyndon Johnson

James 1:27 "Pure and undefiled religion before God the Father is this: to look after orphans and widows in their distress and to keep oneself unstained from the world."

On August 6, 1965, Lyndon Johnson signed the Voting Rights Act into law. This legislation aimed to tear down the obstacles that were in place against African Americans who wanted to vote. This was a serious problem. For example, voter turnout for African Americans was 6% in Mississippi in 1964, so obviously something needed to be done.

Today's verse indicates that we are called to help those who are not empowered to help themselves. Certainly some would argue that this is our calling as believers, and we should not absolve ourselves of responsibility by handing the job over to the government. Nevertheless, we can see the principle in action in what the government did. We should not be legalists when it comes to living out what the Bible says. I do *not* mean we should ignore what it says; I mean we should not confine ourselves to specific examples of behaviors and ignore the general principles that are being conveyed. Specifically, in this context I mean if James says we should take care of widows and orphans, then we should help out other groups that cannot help themselves.

We are called to help people when we have the power to do so, be it in the workplace, in our families, in our neighborhoods, or in our churches. Who can we help today?

Day 97

James Madison

Proverbs 19:20 "Listen to counsel and receive instruction so that you may be wise later in life."

On August 7, 2019, I learned something that very much surprised me. James Madison, who eventually became close friends with Ben Franklin, at one point thought the famous patriot, diplomat, and inventor was a British spy. In a letter to a friend in 1775, Madison wrote, "The bare suspicion of his guilt amounts nearly to a proof of its reality."

Thus, not only was Madison way off base, but he had also nearly convinced himself that Franklin should be considered guilty until he could prove himself innocent.

Madison was a brilliant man, but this demonstrates that even really smart people are not always right. To put a finer point on it, there are times when smart people think dumb things. For example, until I was in my thirties, I used the words "across" and "acrost" interchangeably, which would be fine, except "acrost" is not actually a word. Of course, this example only works if I am a smart person, so, um, let's move on.

It is helpful to get input from other people at times. We benefit from godly counsel, and we ignore it at our peril. We need to be humble enough to accept advice from others. James Madison was brilliant, so if he could have bad ideas, what hope do the rest of us have? Even he needed someone to help him process some of his ideas. If you don't currently have someone providing godly counsel in your life, pray that God will direct you to that person, starting today.

Day 98

Richard Nixon

Romans 14:12 "So then, each of us will give an account of himself to God."

On August 8, 1974, President Nixon announced his resignation. He tried to make it sound noble, but he was quitting so he wouldn't suffer the indignity of getting thrown out of office over the Watergate scandal. At the time, people believed that Nixon didn't know about the plan to break into the Democratic National Committee's headquarters to spy on them. Most investigators believed that Nixon was only guilty of the cover-up that took place after the fact.

When some of Nixon's men got arrested, others on Nixon's team funneled money to them. One of those responsible for the payments said he was motivated by compassion for these zealous supporters who had gotten carried away in the heat of the election and now faced financial difficulties.

When word of the payments got out, however, many believed the White House was paying these men not to cooperate with prosecutors when questions were asked about who approved their operation. Nixon obtained some of the money that was used to pay off those who had been arrested. It sure looked like a cover-up.

Sometimes we face the same kind of temptation. We've done something we know we shouldn't have, and rather than own it, we try to cover up our sin.

Nixon was never accountable to anyone. He never admitted to any wrongdoing, and even after he resigned, Ford pardoned him, so he never faced judgment. At least, he never did in this life.

They say the First Rule of Holes is this: When you are in one, stop digging. Some of us are in a hole. We need to stop digging. We need to be accountable to someone now, or we're going to be held accountable by Someone later.

Day 99

George Washington

Matthew 25:23 "His master said to him, 'Well done, good and faithful servant! You were faithful over a few things; I will put you in charge of many things. Share your master's joy.'"

Bootstrapping is an awesome quality. Basically, it means getting oneself out of a situation by using the resources on hand. Instead of hoping that someone else will come in and give us what we want, or lamenting our misfortune and what we lack, to bootstrap is to take what we do have and make the best of it. It is a term based on the old saying, "Pull yourself up by your own bootstraps."

On August 9, 2019, I learned that George Washington's personal library consisted of over 900 books. If you add in pamphlets and other reading materials, he had more than 1200 separate things to read at his house.

He had very little formal education, but he spent the rest of his life trying to make up for it. Instead of feeling sorry for himself, or engaging in sour grapes and saying that education was overrated, Washington invested in reading materials so he could improve his level of understanding of the world around him. And his library was not just for show. Washington turned himself into an avid reader.

We can lament the things we were not blessed with, we can be jealous about opportunities that others received, or we can do the best we can with what we have. We are not going to be judged by what kind of stewards we were of someone else's gifts; what matters is what we do with our own. If we are still breathing—and if you are reading this, let's assume that you are—God has given you something, some talent, resource, or time, to use for His glory. Are we making the most of what God has given us? Let's pray about that today.

Day 100

Andrew Jackson

Psalm 4:4 "Be angry and do not sin; on your bed, reflect in your heart and be still."

Andrew Jackson had a bit of a temper. One day he was in court (before being a soldier and a president, he was a lawyer), and his opponent basically made him look stupid. The opposition lawyer, the peculiarly named Waightsell Avery, was really only arguing the law. Jackson, though, had been an indifferent student, and even upon developing an interest in lawyering, he wasn't exactly Type A about learning the ins and outs of jurisprudence.

Despite the genuine disadvantage he faced, Jackson refused to accept the idea that his opponent was just doing his job. Jackson decided that Avery was trying to mock and humiliate him. On August 12, 1788, the future seventh President of the United States wrote out a formal challenge on a page in a law book and threw it (the single page or the whole book, the story varies) at his opponent. Avery tried to shrug it off, but Jackson insisted. There was going to be a duel.

Fortunately, by the time of the event, Jackson had calmed down, so both men simply fired their guns harmlessly in the air, and honor was served.

Jackson was a tempestuous man, but his anger did not hurt him. This time.

Anger is not a sin; it's an emotion. That said, sometimes it leads us to sin. For some, it's a bigger deal than it is for others, but however often it happens, we should pray for grace when we get angry.

Day 101

John Kennedy

Exodus 20:17 "Do not covet your neighbor's house. Do not covet your neighbor's wife, his male or female servant, his ox or donkey, or anything that belongs to your neighbor."

It can be tempting to think other people have it nicer than we do. From the outside looking in, it might be easy to imagine that John Kennedy's life was perfect. He came from a rich family. He grew up in a house full of people. He was good looking and charismatic. He seemed to have it all. Who wouldn't want to trade places with him and his perfect life?

Tragedy struck, however, on August 12, 1944. His older brother, Joe Junior, was killed. It was a shock to the family. The loss was tragic. Joe was the one who was being groomed for a career in politics, but now John would have to carry that burden and all the expectations that went with it. And that, of course, was not the only weight he was carrying. Part of the family's wealth came from John Kennedy's dad selling bootleg liquor during Prohibition. Was that embarrassing for John? The future president also had a number of physical ailments that made life difficult.

Envy and jealousy are never good. They demonstrate a lack of love for whomever it is we are jealous of, but there is more to it than that. It demonstrates a desire to play God, really. We think we know enough to say what is best and fairest for us and for others. We don't always know the challenges in someone else's life, but we think we know enough to decide we want what they have. And yet that wasn't God's plan for us or them. We don't fully know what someone else's portion is; we only know what we see. Let us pray today to be content with what God has given us and not covet what He has given someone else.

Day 102

George Washington

Romans 14:13 "Therefore, let us no longer judge one another. Instead decide never to put a stumbling block or pitfall in the way of your brother or sister."

A prominent historian wrote in a book a few years back that George Washington was the only one of our nine slave-owning presidents who freed his slaves. On August 13, 2019, I was reading this, and I actually counted twelve presidents. And I believe one of them only had one slave, and he freed that man.

Nevertheless, Washington went the extra mile on this, and it is worth mentioning in a culture where some want to dismiss Washington as unworthy of any praise because he owned slaves.

Really, though, this isn't about Washington; it's about us. By what standard do we measure other people? Do we condemn them for their imperfections, or do we recognize that everyone has been shaped by their experiences and circumstances?

I absolutely do not mean to downplay the evils of slavery. Being a slave owner is a pretty big "imperfection," to use my own word. But if a person grew up in a society where slave owning was normal and a sign of success, and then that person was able to recognize the evil of it after becoming wildly successful in that system, that means something.

The point is we need to be sensitive to the baggage people are carrying and the circumstances that helped shape them. We need to love people and show a little Christian charity today. This doesn't mean we turn a blind eye to sin; it just means we lead with love over judgment.

Day 103

Jimmy Carter

Romans 16:1-2 "I commend to you our sister Phoebe, who is a servant of the church in Cenchreae. So you should welcome her in the Lord in a manner worthy of the saints and assist her in whatever matter she may require your help. For indeed she has been a benefactor of many—and of me also."

On August 18, 1922, Rosalynn Carter was born.

Her future husband, Jimmy Carter, used to invite her to Cabinet meetings during his presidency. This happened in the 1970s, so it raised eyebrows for a couple of reasons: (1) She was not a senate-approved Cabinet official, and (2) she was "just" the wife of the president, so what did she know?

His explanation: He was going to ask for her opinion on things, so she might as well be as informed as possible. Certainly Jimmy Carter was not the only president to see wisdom in his wife's counsel. Abigail Adams was the only person her husband, John, listened to who he could actually trust, and Franklin Roosevelt had a lot of respect for Eleanor's judgment (if not for his marital bond to her).

Carter, though, was the first president to have his wife attend actual Cabinet meetings. There were some complaints, but probably most of those doing the complaining would have grumbled about something else if not her, politics being what it is.

Speaking of Jimmy Carter respecting his wife's input, does the church need to do a better job at empowering women? Do we welcome women "in a manner worthy of the saints," or do we grudgingly let women do things in the areas where men aren't stepping up? Do we tolerate it when women fill holes in church? That's a thing, but it is not the same as supporting our sisters in Christ.

Day 104

Bill Clinton

John 3:16 "For God loved the world in this way: He gave His one and only Son, so that everyone who believes in Him will not perish but have eternal life."

Bill Clinton experienced his physical birth on August 19, 1946. His spiritual birth took place several years later in 1955. His family did not attend church regularly, but somehow he did. He got himself to church, and he got involved there, even though that was not modeled for him by his family. Better yet, as a nine-year-old, he acknowledged that he was a sinner who needed Christ.

During his presidency, conservatives criticized him for his behavior toward women, and in the wake of #MeToo, some liberals have criticized him, also. How does that impact our understanding of the decision he made as a child? It's not for me to say. But in that moment in time as a nine-year-old, he made a wise decision.

I probably don't need to "John 3:16" you. If you are the kind of person who reads devotionals, then most likely you have already recognized your need for Christ and done something about it.

For that reason, I am actually going in a different direction. My point today is that we cannot expect everyone to have the initiative of a nine-year-old Bill Clinton. Most people won't make it to church on their own.

We *need* to be people who reach out.

We need to be people who go out.

Let us pray today that we would have a heart of compassion for those who need the Lord.

Day 105

Dwight Eisenhower

Romans 8:28 "We know that all things work together for the good of those who love God, who are called according to His purpose."

On August 20, 1901, Dwight "Ike" Eisenhower wrote a series of letters to Kansas Senator Joseph Bristow. Ike sought Bristow's help in getting into one of the military academies. Ike's first choice was the Naval Academy, but they rejected him.

While Ike was disappointed over this, things worked out pretty well for him in the US Army during a career which spanned from 1915 to 1953. During part of that time, Eisenhower, of course, oversaw American operations in the European Theater of World War Two, which led to a two-term stint as president.

It is hard to imagine that Ike could have had an equally big impact with a career in the US Navy. I mean, technically it's possible that his Navy career could have been as great or greater, but it is also technically possible that I could star in a Broadway show.

I'd say both scenarios are equally unlikely.

Anyway, Ike wanted the Navy first, but the Army was a better fit for him, and it allowed him to better serve America. So it is for us. Sometimes we have big plans, but things go awry. It doesn't mean we failed. *Maybe* there is something bigger for us. God doesn't always promise us something bigger around the corner, but He does ultimately promise us something better. As my friend, Donny Wadley, said to me, "Do you really think that the God who sent Jesus to die on the cross for you doesn't care about your circumstances now? That doesn't make sense." God is at work in our lives for our ultimate good. Let us find comfort in that today.

Day 106

Gerald Ford

Proverbs 24:10 "If you do nothing in a difficult time, your strength is limited."

On September 5, 1975, a woman tried to shoot Gerald Ford. She didn't succeed. The woman who tried to shoot him 17 days later didn't get it done either. Did Ford deserve to be shot at by these women? Probably not, but when you are in leadership, or when you take a stand on, well, anything, sometimes people will attack you. Usually not with a gun, but you know the person who coined the phrase "sticks and stones may break my bones, but words will never hurt me?" That person was wrong. It hurts to be attacked, even just verbally. But it doesn't mean we are doing something wrong.

It might mean we're wrong about something, so we need accountability, as mentioned elsewhere, but sometimes opposition comes with the territory, and we have to deal with it. Unfortunately, some of us deal with it by not making any hard decisions. We play it safe; we don't rock the boat. Of course, refusing to make a decision is a decision in and of itself, but for the faint of heart, it feels easier to push a problem down the road than it does to face it today.

Bold and decisive leadership might invite criticism, but so does weakness. Avoiding criticism really doesn't belong on the agenda of a leader.

We should pray for the intestinal fortitude today to do the right thing, not the easy thing.

Day 107

1 Samuel 16:7 "But the Lord said to Samuel, 'Do not look at his appearance or his stature because I have rejected him. Humans do not see what the Lord sees, for humans see what is visible, but the Lord sees the heart.'"

On September 8, 1883, Theodore Roosevelt visited North Dakota on a hunting expedition. Shortly thereafter, he bought land and became a rancher. The cowboys who worked his land had a hard time taking him seriously at first. To them, he was an over-educated skinny guy with thick glasses who used words that were too fancy for life on the range. He was a rich city slicker who wanted to play at being a cowboy.

Nevertheless, he won them over because he was tough, he loved to work hard, and he was fearless.

Here's the thing: They weren't wrong about him. Everything they thought was correct. But the problem with judging the bookish man by his cover was that they didn't see the other qualities that were there.

It's actually human nature to make snap judgments about a lot of what we encounter in life. Everything after that is confirmation bias. As we process new information, we believe that which supports our initial judgment, and we are skeptical about that which contradicts it. But we don't have to just rely on our human nature.

We need to lean on the Holy Spirit, and we need to show the grace that was shown to us. Sometimes people can surprise us if we give them a chance. Let us pray today that we will give someone a chance whom we might otherwise dismiss prematurely.

Day 108

Millard Fillmore

Isaiah 2:12 "For a day belonging to the Lord of Armies is coming against all that is proud and lofty, against all that is lifted up—it will be humbled."

On September 9, 1850, Millard Fillmore said (inaccurately as it turned out) "The long agony is over." He was referring to the huge and divisive debate over slavery. Regarding the matter at hand, and the context of Fillmore's quotation, Congress had just hammered out a huge compromise that was meant to appeal to different groups in the country. This was discussed early in our book on Day 15.

Of course, Fillmore was wrong: The agony was not over. It got much worse. Bleeding Kansas, where people killed each other over the slavery issue later in the 1850s, was bad enough. The Civil War of the 1860s was exponentially worse.

Fillmore was a reasonably smart and very successful politician, but he totally misread this situation. In order for us to walk in humility, we should not be so quick to think we have all the answers. It is so easy to pop off with an opinion when we only have a partial understanding of a situation.

Part of the arrogance, too, was found in a plan that offered a way forward for the country, but it did nothing for the millions of American slaves. The arrogant can easily prove themselves indifferent to the suffering of people who don't matter to them.

Let's learn from Fillmore and offer our opinions with care and humility today. And let's make decisions that are characterized by compassion.

Day 109

James Madison

Leviticus 19:34 "You will regard the alien who resides with you as the native-born among you. You are to love him as yourself, for you were aliens in the land of Egypt; I am the Lord your God."

On September 15, 1794, James Madison married late and above his station. Dolley was young, attractive, and charming, and…well…those were not things they had in common. Dolley was twenty-six when they married; James was forty-two. She was vivacious and outgoing, and he was sickly and shy. But despite these differences, they were both smart and interesting people. And they were also both surprisingly brave. Dolley risked her safety to save a painting of George Washington as the British were torching Washington, DC, during the War of 1812. When James was a young man, he tried to serve in the Virginia militia, despite his small frame and poor health. Ultimately, he had to drop out, but he gave it his all.

If James and Dolley had focused solely on what they did not have in common, they probably would not have gotten together. Or perhaps they did focus on their differences and realized that the other was strong where they were lacking. Thus, they could do more together than apart.

How do we handle it when we encounter people different than us? I'm not saying we should marry them, but maybe we should not be so quick to be uncomfortable. Prejudice takes a lot of forms. Sometimes it's racial, but not always. There are Christians who believe passionately that racism is a sin (because it is), but some of these same Christians will go out of their way to not associate with someone who has different politics or preferences. We need to not be thrown so easily by personal differences—we can love people anyway. We are called to love people anyway.

Day 110

Abraham Lincoln

1 Samuel 13:14A "But now your reign will not endure. The Lord has found a man after His own heart…"

On September 17, 1862, the Battle of Antietam took place. It lasted only one day, and it ended in a stalemate, so one might be tempted to overlook it as inconsequential in the Civil War were it not for one thing: it was the bloodiest day of the war with more than 20,000 men getting wounded. Many died. Countless more were traumatized by what they experienced that day.

After such a horrible battle with nothing gained from a strategic or even just a morale-building standpoint, Abraham Lincoln struggled with a difficult question: On whose side was God? Lincoln had wanted to believe that God favored the Union. Lincoln wanted to preserve the Union, because he knew that Europe was watching to see if this experiment in liberty and democracy could work. If our country fell apart, then European governments would have an excuse not to extend greater freedoms to their own people. Lincoln thought God would be on the side of freedom from oppression.

After Antietam, the president was not so sure.

What humility! Lincoln had his agenda, and he thought it was a good, even noble, one. But after this battle, Lincoln found himself wondering about God's agenda. We would do well to follow in Lincoln's footsteps today. If you read devotionals, there's a fair to middling chance you want to live a life that is pleasing to God. I know I do. Perhaps like me, you try to figure out what you can do to serve His agenda. But there are times when what seems like a righteous agenda to us might only be the second-best scenario (and maybe not even that). We would do well to ask ourselves periodically if we are on God's side in a given situation.

Day 111

George Washington

Psalm 20:7 "Some take pride in chariots, and others in horses, but we take pride in the name of the Lord our God."

George Washington's Farewell Address was published in a Philadelphia newspaper on September 19, 1796, announcing the end of his presidency early the next year. He had been a leader in the nation on and off since 1754, and now he was leaving the public arena for good.

Though some newspaper writers and politicians had begun to criticize the first president, he was still incredibly popular with the majority of the country. It wasn't just his tall, strong physicality or his unfailing personal rectitude and dignity that made him a beloved figure either. There was also the little matter of his improbable victory in the Revolutionary War against what was considered the strongest military in the world.

Besides all of that, Washington was trusted to hold the leading office in the country because he was...safe. Many Americans were concerned that putting too much power in the hands of one government official might corrupt that person and turn him into a tyrant. Such a person might try and make himself king. Washington was seen as safe because he had already foiled a military plot to install him as a dictator. Also, he had no biological children, and it seemed unlikely that a man his age would make himself king, if he did not have an automatic heir in waiting.

Washington was a great pick to lead the country, but now it was time for him to retire. We cannot fall into the trap of putting our trust in people, because all of us are temporary. We need to put our trust in the Lord. Let's pray for the faith to do that today.

Day 112

Chester Arthur

Luke 9:25 "For what does it benefit someone if he gains the whole world, and yet loses or forfeits himself?"

As discussed earlier, James Garfield was shot, and in September 1881, he finally succumbed to his wounds. The next day, September 20, was the first full day of the Chester Arthur presidency.

Largely forgotten today, Arthur served honorably as president for almost three and a half years. Since he hadn't been chosen by his party in the first place, it is not shocking that the Republicans went in a different direction in 1884, but Arthur would have served four more years if he had been offered the chance.

Candidates back then typically did not go around and ask for votes—most of them considered that undignified—but Arthur at least made sure people knew he was ready, willing, and able. The problem with Arthur was he might have tried a little too hard to please everybody. He spoke of progressive reforms, but he did not really fight for them. Thus, he did not do enough to woo progressives, but he did too much as far as conservatives were concerned. He was not unpalatable as a candidate, but both wings of the Republican Party felt they could do better.

And what of us? Are we firm in our convictions and loving in our demeanor, or do we teeter to one side or the other? Are we, like Chester Arthur, so concerned with being accepted that we don't take a firm stand for our beliefs? This dying world needs difference-makers, not fence straddlers. Which one are we going to be today? Let us pray for ears that strain to hear the applause of Christ rather than the applause of those around us.

Day 113

Dwight Eisenhower

Matthew 21:12 "Jesus went into the temple and threw out all those buying and selling. He overturned the tables of the money changers and the chairs of those selling doves."

On September 23, 1957, President Dwight D. "Ike" Eisenhower sent the US Army into Arkansas because the governor there defied a Supreme Court ruling and tried to maintain racial segregation in a high school in Little Rock. The governor was using the National Guard to thwart the will of the federal government, and Ike was not going to put up with that.

After guiding Allied Forces in the European Theater to victory in World War Two, Ike was accustomed to having people follow orders. The United States Supreme Court had issued its ruling, "separate is not equal," and the president expected the states to follow one hundred fifty years of judicial precedent and obey it.

The Governor of Arkansas planted his flag on a hill called "racism," so Ike sent in the Army to make sure African American kids could go to a previously all-white school without fear of attack.

The moral of the story: Sometimes we need to make a bold stand. Christians are supposed to be nice, we're called to love people, and we are expected to get along peacefully with others. But Jesus didn't get the temple cleared by singing a praise chorus. There are times when we are called to be tough-minded. Most of us are willing to fight when it comes to our perceived rights and reputation, but those things aren't what prompted Jesus to clear the temple. The One I am called to fight for isn't me; He's One who is greater than me. Let's pray for the courage to stand up for Him today.

Day 114

Richard Nixon and Dwight Eisenhower

Luke 23:34A "Then Jesus said, 'Father, forgive them, because they do not know what they are doing.'"

On September 23, 1952, Republican vice-presidential candidate Richard Nixon saved his political career (temporarily) with the "Checkers Speech."

What happened was this: Fresh off winning World War Two, Ike was so popular that it put Democrats in a pickle. They didn't think they could win the race if they focused on him, so instead they decided to go after his running mate, Nixon, whom they accused of getting bribes by means of a secret slush fund. Nixon got on TV, which was new, and he talked at length about his personal finances, which was unheard of back then. Nixon denied making any undeclared profit from his political career—with one key exception. He admitted to taking a gift recently while out campaigning—it was a little dog that one of his girls named "Checkers." Heartstrings were tugged and Nixon was saved.

Meanwhile, Ike had been encouraged by his advisors to throw Nixon overboard. Eisenhower didn't really know the man, so there was no personal commitment, but Ike decided to let the situation unfold, and when Nixon saved himself, the issue went away.

But Nixon was a master at holding on to resentment. Some have suggested that Nixon got involved in the Watergate cover-up because he wanted to support his people better than Ike supported him. Resentment is a cancer that leads to bad things. If you've got it, let it go. If it's too hard for you to let it go, pray for the Holy Spirit to move in your heart.

Day 115

Grover Cleveland

1 Corinthians 7:35 "I am saying this for your own benefit, not to put a restraint on you, but to promote what is proper and so that you may be devoted to the Lord without distraction."

On September 25, 1894, President Grover Cleveland pardoned all of the convicted polygamists in Utah. This was the next step in the process of Utah becoming a state and the Latter Day Saints trying to be acceptable to mainstream America.

Four years earlier, the leader of the Latter Day Saints had shared a new revelation: God no longer favored polygamy. Utah would not be voted in as a state until the LDS (Mormon) Church repudiated polygamy, so it did. Cleveland, building on actions started by his predecessor, Benjamin Harrison, decided to put the matter thoroughly in the rear view mirror by wiping the slate clean. As long as convicted polygamists promised to be monogamous moving forward, they were freed from prison, and their rights were restored.

The Point? There isn't one; this was just interesting. Don't get me wrong, polygamy is bad, but I don't think I need to make that point in this devotional. In our context here, it's just an interesting story. It is not a bad story to tell; it's just...not helpful in a devotional.

How often do we distract ourselves with things that aren't bad but also aren't helpful, even with our church programs? We need to be better stewards of our resources than that. Let's focus today on being productive for the Kingdom of God, and not being so distracted by the mundane and unimportant.

Day 116

Theodore Roosevelt

John 11:43-44 "After He said this, He shouted with a loud voice, 'Lazarus, come out!' The dead man came out bound hand and foot with linen strips and with his face wrapped in a cloth. Jesus said to them, 'Unwrap him and let him go.'"

Young Theodore Roosevelt went off to Harvard on September 27, 1876. When he wasn't celebrating the nation's centennial birthday that semester, he spent his time making a poor first impression on people. He weighed only 125 pounds spread across his five feet, eight-inch frame, and he had squinty eyes behind thick glasses to go along with a weird speaking voice.

There was nothing about him that made people think, "That guy could be President of the United States someday!" And, yet, that is who he became. He was smart, fearless, and charming, and those things tended to win people over.

Likewise for us, we might not be overly impressed with who we have been so far. We might be a little too aware of other people's strengths, as we measure them against our weaknesses. But maybe, as with Theodore Roosevelt, when people look close enough, they will see some good qualities in us.

If Jesus could raise Lazarus from the dead, what might He do through us, if we would only believe? If you are reading this—and, um, you clearly are—your story is not finished yet. What are you going to do with that truth? I would recommend that you lean into it. Pray that God will give you faith—not in yourself, but in Him—to see that He can and will use you for something special.

Day 117

Harry Truman

Mark 16:15 "Then He said to them, 'Go into all the world and preach the gospel to all creation.'"

We talked about the Korean War on Day 77. Harry Truman decided to support the United Nations' operation to save South Korea from the invasion of Communist North Korea. The mission was a success; the North Korean Army was quickly pushed north of the line that divided the Korean Peninsula. But the American general in charge of the UN operation, Douglas MacArthur, was not content with this victory. He wanted to drive the Communists out of Korea altogether and thus reunite the nation. On September 27, 1950, Truman authorized MacArthur to go north of the 38th Parallel.

It was a daring move. It went beyond what the United Nations had agreed to, and it went beyond what Truman had originally presented to Congress and the American people. But at the height of the Cold War between the democracies and communism, there was a lot of support for this initially. And it was successful. MacArthur's forces drove the North Korean Army out of their country. On paper, it looked like Korea was reunified and MacArthur and Truman were heroes, but such things don't last forever.

It got China involved in the Korean War. The Red Army steamrolled into the peninsula, and Allied forces were pushed back down to the 38th Parallel. All that extra fighting had gained us nothing except more dead and wounded service personnel. We lost our focus on the original mission and suffered for it. How many of our churches, and us individually, have done the same? We get distracted from our primary mission of making disciples by something that sounds good but is not the primary mission. Let's pray together that we can keep our focus on that which is our true calling: making disciples.

Day 118

George Washington and James Madison

John 1:45-46 "Philip found Nathanael and told him, 'We have found the one Moses wrote about in the law (and so did the prophets): Jesus the son of Joseph, from Nazareth.' 'Can anything good come out of Nazareth?' Nathanael asked him. 'Come and see,' Philip answered."

On October 1, 1789, James Madison spent the day with George Washington. Their friendship would be strained in later years over political differences, and the influence of Thomas Jefferson on Madison, but Madison's loyalty to Washington never really died.

When the friendship between the first and fourth presidents was at its strongest, which was the case in 1789—the first year of the United States' government and Washington's presidency—both men benefitted greatly. Washington had an unofficial advisor, who happened to be the country's foremost expert on political science and a loyal advocate in the House of Representatives. Madison enjoyed direct communication with and influence on the head of the executive branch, the reputation-enhancement of being associated with the most popular man in the country, and a chance to learn from a man with unparalleled leadership skills.

Cultivating positive relationships with great people can be a tremendous benefit for us as Christian disciples. Who are the best people we know? We need to figure out how to spend time with them. And, of course, the other side of that coin is we have to figure out, prayerfully, how to be those kinds of people, so we can be a resource for others.

Day 119

Ronald Reagan

Psalm 35:18 "I will praise You in the great assembly; I will exalt You among many people."

Ronald Reagan was an unlikely choice to win a lot of support from evangelical Christians in 1980. Reagan was divorced, and we had never had a divorced president before. Speaking of which, when he was governor of California, Reagan signed into law the first no-fault divorce legislation. Finally, Reagan's opponent, Jimmy Carter, was a devout Baptist who taught Sunday School and spoke of being "born again."

Nevertheless, many Christians did flock to Reagan. For a lot of them, it had as much or more to do with politics than faith. Times were tough in the country and around the world, and Reagan was offering something different than Carter.

For others, though, there were things Reagan said about matters of faith that resonated. Reagan spoke to the National Religious Broadcasters on October 3, 1980 and advocated school prayer. He also expressed his belief that the Bible had the answers to the world's problems.

Is it any wonder that so many Christians voted for the guy?

Sure, it was easy for Reagan to be outspoken about the faith in front of that particular "great assembly," but Reagan knew his words would spread outside that assembly, and he still spoke up boldly for God, prayer, and the Bible.

What do we think about prayer and the Bible? Do we want prayer in schools, but ignore it in our own lives? Would we agree that the Bible has a lot of answers, and yet fail to read it regularly ourselves? Let us rededicate ourselves today to be people of prayer and Bible study.

Day 120

Rutherford Hayes

Proverbs 26:13 "The slacker says, 'There's a lion in the road—a lion in the public square.'"

On October 4, 1822, Rutherford Hayes was born. His father had died a few months before this.

Hayes had quite a life. He graduated as valedictorian of his college class at nineteen years of age. He went on to Harvard and got a law degree. He later joined the Army and rose to the rank of major general. Hayes served in the House of Representatives briefly before serving three terms as Governor of Ohio. Finally, Hayes was elected President of the United States in 1876.

Actually, maybe he wasn't. The election results were bitterly disputed, but Hayes ended up getting the job, fairly or otherwise. For what it's worth, there is no evidence that Hayes was personally involved in anything fishy.

Today's Scripture is one of my favorites in all the Old Testament. It's a little subtle, but it makes a great point. It's kind of like my writing, except that it's subtle, and it makes a great point.

Anyway, the point here is that we always have reasons for why we don't accomplish more. The slacker is worried about the lion in the street. One person might lament the lack of a strong father figure, another person might complain that his parents never encouraged a solid work ethic, and a third person could point out that if her parents had more money, she could have gotten into a better college. If I were better looking, I would be more popular. If I were more charismatic, I would have had a successful job interview. At some point we have to stop making excuses and just get stuff done. Rutherford Hayes had a great reason to not accomplish much, but he did anyway. Let's not make excuses today.

Day 121

Richard Nixon

Titus 2:1 "But you are to proclaim things consistent with sound teaching."

On October 9, 1933, young Richard Nixon wrote a paper for school discussing his religious beliefs. More than forty years later, he referred to those writings to describe his beliefs in his memoirs.

For Nixon, the important takeaway about Jesus is that He set an example for us to hold in our hearts and learn and grow from. This, said Nixon, was more important than whether or not the actual Resurrection occurred.

This is nice. Nixon gives us a non-threatening Jesus who makes no real demands. You won't get any of that "narrow is the way" stuff from Nixon's Jesus. The Jesus portrayed in Nixon's account is a warm, fuzzy Jesus who offers us a bunch of religious platitudes and nice bromides that we can choose from like we're at a buffet.

But that is not Christianity.

That said, in our world today, it is a type of faith that many people find attractive. Thus, we must be vigilant so this sort of philosophy doesn't creep into our thinking. Jesus is not primarily a role model for us; He's the Savior of our souls. You probably think of Him as Savior if you are reading this book, but sometimes even stout believers start to entertain wrong thinking. Jesus isn't just Someone who can teach us how to grow as people; He's the Lamb of God who was sacrificed for our sins. Let us pray that today we will be fueled by that sacrifice and face the world with our faith intact.

Day 122

Theodore Roosevelt

Hebrews 12:11 "No discipline seems enjoyable at the time, but painful. Later on, however, it yields the peaceful fruit of righteousness to those who have been trained by it."

On October 14, 1912, Theodore Roosevelt was shot while campaigning for president. The shooter was an anarchist who was bothered by the idea of Roosevelt potentially serving a third term (presidents were not yet limited to two terms).

Roosevelt said, "It takes more than that to kill a bull moose" and went ahead and gave the speech he had scheduled.

Now, in the interest of historical accuracy, I must point out that the bullet was slowed down by the jacket he was wearing, had to tear through the case Roosevelt kept his glasses in, and further had to cut through a copy of his speech that was folded up and nestled in his jacket pocket.

Still, it was a bullet, and it went into his body. The good news was the speech was fifty pages, so there was a lot of material to slow the bullet down. The bad news was his speech was fifty pages, and it took him eighty minutes to read it. By the time his talk was over, his shirt was soaked in blood.

This was the moment Roosevelt had spent his whole life preparing, pushing, and disciplining himself for. To him, life was a test, and he was determined to always pass the test. His quotation, which epitomized his outlook on life, is "Pray not for lighter burdens, but for stronger backs."

Honestly? I've been known to pray for a lighter burden or two. But it is the burdens we carry that make us grow as disciples. Hard times can help us develop perseverance and empathy. Let us pray today that we can learn something from our burdens.

Day 123

Andrew Johnson

Colossians 4:6 "Let your speech always be gracious, seasoned with salt, so that you may know how you should answer each person."

On October 15, 1845, Andrew Johnson launched into a spirited defense of his religious beliefs. Johnson, a Democrat, was accused by the enemy Whig Party of all kinds of non-Christian things.

The future seventeenth president used logic to defend himself. He pointed out that it was impossible that he was both an "avowed atheist" and a "secret infidel," as his enemies asserted. He argued, correctly, that if he had avowed his atheism, then his infidelity would not be much of a secret.

He also used Scripture to defend himself and describe his beliefs.

Johnson tied his understanding of Christianity into his patriotic love of American democracy, but let's not open that can of worms.

The point of today's devotional is not to answer the question of Johnson's faith, though it is interesting that he is one of the very few presidents who never joined a church. The point for today is to raise some interesting questions about us. What would our enemies say about our faith? If someone publicly expressed doubt about our faith, how would we respond? Would we get angry or defensive? If we needed to explain our faith could we?

We should pray about these things today and ponder what our responses could be.

Day 124

Abraham Lincoln

Philippians 4:5 "Let your graciousness be known to everyone. The Lord is near."

On October 16, 1854, in a debate with Senator Stephen Douglass, Lincoln said something remarkably gracious. While discussing slavery to an audience in Peoria, Illinois, Lincoln might have been tempted to pander to the northern crowd and say some derogatory things about southern slave owners. But Lincoln demonstrated a good understanding of human nature. He said that though the South supported slavery, if it had not existed up to that point, southerners would not support starting it in 1854. And he went on to say that if Illinois had slavery in 1854, the people there would not be so quick to give it up.

Lincoln was not downplaying the evils of slavery; he was simply pointing out that northerners were not inherently superior to southerners.

Are we gracious in our comments and thoughts about those who struggle with certain moral issues, or are we quick to judge and condemn? It would be easy for me to condemn someone, for example, who struggles with a gambling addiction, because I have never felt the pull of that particular temptation. I'm more sensitive, though, with those who struggle with forgiveness, because there have been pains that were difficult for me to let go of.

We should pray today for the same kind of sensitivity Lincoln displayed when it comes to having a merciful and charitable heart toward others.

Day 125

Benjamin Harrison

Colossians 4:2 "Devote yourselves to prayer; stay alert in it with thanksgiving."

On October 19, 1752, there was an article in a newspaper about Ben Franklin's experiment with electricity. It would be a while before this development paid off in the form of electric lights in the White House. In fact, those were not installed until 1891.

But these new lights did not do as much good as they could have because Benjamin Harrison was afraid his light switch would electrocute him. This electric power was at his disposal, but he didn't use it. It did not matter what the benefits of electric-powered light were. It did not matter that Harrison could be productive for more hours of the day, and thus have better served the country, because he did not take advantage of what he had.

Are we similarly afflicted when it comes to prayer? Most of us usually aren't afraid of it, though I have known people who avoided certain prayers because they were afraid of what God might tell them to do. At least most of the time we don't fear prayer, but the result is the same: We don't do it, so the power that is there is lost to us.

This theme has been repeated in this book, because it is so critically important to believers. Too many of us consistently neglect prayer, and it makes us spiritually weak when it comes to our walk as disciples, and it makes us ineffectual in our impact on a world that is going to Hell without Christ.

I urge you to put this book down, get on your knees, and pray right now.

Day 126

Woodrow Wilson

Matthew 10:16 "Look, I'm sending you out like sheep among wolves. Therefore, be as shrewd as serpents and as innocent as doves."

On October 20, 1910, Woodrow Wilson submitted his resignation as President of Princeton. Wilson successfully ran for Governor of New Jersey, and now it was time to transition. The governorship became a stepping stone to the presidency.

Expressing oneself in politics, though, is different than communicating in the world of academia. While lamenting the ridiculous things some people say, Wilson said something to the effect of "If there is one good thing about tobacco, at least it gives a man a moment to collect his thoughts before he speaks."

A newspaper that didn't like Wilson's politics decided to spin his comments to say, "Wilson says tobacco makes you smarter."

There are times when people take our words out of context, and sometimes they kind of do it on purpose. Since we can't change other people, we need to be especially diligent about how we communicate. Do we say things that allow people to put a stumbling block in front of the gospel? Will people tune me out if I say something mean, or insensitive, or politically volatile? What will happen when I try to communicate the gospel to them? Am I sacrificing the gospel because I want to get a load off my chest about something less than the gospel? Let us pray for wisdom in what we say and how we say it. If people want to twist our words to embarrass us, let's at least make it kind of hard for them. Let's pray for wisdom today when it comes to what we say.

Day 127

James Madison

Acts 16:6 "They went through the region of Phrygia and Galatia; they had been forbidden by the Holy Spirit to speak the word to Asia."

On October 22, 1746, a charter authorizing the creation of the College of New Jersey (later Princeton University) was issued. This school played a pivotal role in the life of young James Madison.

As mentioned earlier, he tried to serve in the Virginia militia, but he was too small and sickly for military life. Rather than stay at home on the plantation and feel sorry for himself—rather than allowing himself to be defined by what he could not do—Madison instead went to college and developed his mind. He graduated and then stayed an extra year studying Hebrew.

Why Hebrew? Well, he had considered a career in the ministry, but he had already changed course by this point, so his primary motivation was probably not spiritual. The Old Testament is a religious text, but it also lays out a bunch of laws for governing a nation. James Madison had become quite interested in political theory. He developed a voracious appetite for books on the law and the histories of democracies and republics. He would become America's leading political scientist, and he went on to earn the label "Father of the Constitution."

How about us? Do we spend a lot of mental energy in frustrations over things that did not work out for us? Do we need to instead acknowledge that some doors are closed for a reason and refocus our energy on a new way to serve, to make a difference, to have an impact? Instead of lamenting what God hasn't given us, we should accept that He has closed the door for a reason, or at least allowed it to be closed, and we need to figure out how to get to the door He has left open.

Day 128

Herbert Hoover

Romans 8:37 "No, in all these things we are more than conquerors through Him who loved us."

On October 22, 1914, Herbert Hoover successfully concluded negotiations with Britain and Germany—two leading opponents in World War One—that allowed Hoover to begin to bring in food for starving Belgians.

World War Two ended on May 8, 1945. The next year, Herbert Hoover was there coordinating shipments of food into Europe to deal with a post-war famine. Years of bombings and battles had destroyed a lot of farmland, and a lot of farmers were killed, too. Hoover won humanitarian awards after both World Wars for his efforts to feed the hungry.

For many Americans who learn about Herbert Hoover in school, all they remember is he was the do-nothing president who preceded FDR. Roosevelt was the one who did all the programs to try and help people survive the Great Depression; Hoover was the mean guy who sat back and didn't care.

At least, that's what some people think, if they think about him at all.

In real life, though, Hoover was an extremely intelligent and compassionate man who used his disciplined and organized mind to figure out how to get food to the needy. He saved countless lives.

Sometimes people don't see us for who we really are; they see us as something less. Sometimes we see ourselves the same way. For those of us in Christ, we truly are more than conquerors. Let us remember today to seek our identities, and our sense of self-worth, in Him. We are children of the King, and we are going to live forever.

Let's go out and seize the day!

Day 129

John Adams

Proverbs 27:4 "Fury is cruel, and anger a flood, but who can withstand jealousy?"

On October 24, 1800, Alexander Hamilton published a pamphlet telling the world what he thought of John Adams. Hamilton, the founder of the Federalist Party, was frustrated because he wasn't a viable candidate for president due to some of his personal baggage. Consequently, Adams was the man in the White House, but Hamilton thought Adams should defer to him anyway.

When Adams did not subordinate himself to the all-mighty Hamilton, the fiery Hamilton put out his pamphlet on Adams.

Spoiler alert: It was something less than flattering.

Hamilton no doubt enjoyed getting a load off his chest, and Adams—for all of his virtue and brilliance—could be insufferably irritating, but the pamphlet was a disaster for both men. Hamilton's star had faded, but he was still popular enough to hurt's Adams' re-election efforts. Then, resentment over Hamilton's lack of party loyalty, along with a few other issues, ruined Hamilton's chances of making a comeback and taking Adams' spot as the leading Federalist.

The Democratic-Republicans, and specifically Thomas Jefferson, took over the White House.

The point: Jealousy is not a good core value when pursuing career goals.

More to the point: Because jealousy is so poisonous for both the target and the source, we are commanded to have nothing to do with it. If jealousy is a weight we are carrying, we need to pray for the grace to let it go today.

Day 130

John Adams

Ephesians 5:21 "Submitting to one another in the fear of Christ."

John Adams began a great marriage with Abigail on October 25, 1764. She was brilliant, devoted, and longsuffering—we know this last one because she was married to John.

John Adams believed himself to be brilliant, but he was occasionally unaware of his flaws. He could at times be brutally honest about some of his weaknesses while painfully oblivious to others. And he was so accepting of his self-view as a great man that he tended to brush off the attempts of others to show him the errors of his ways.

Abigail, though, was not so easily dismissed. She knew John too well, and they both knew she loved him too much to let him get away with being, well, himself. For example, John once made an unkind comment about George Washington's lack of a formal education. Abigail chided her husband and pointed out that Washington should be credited for his almost unparalleled character and integrity.

We all benefit from loving accountability. At least, we could benefit, if we are open to it. Many of us are tempted to play the "you're not the boss of me" card, but the reality is we are sinners in need of correction. There are times when the Lord speaks through others to straighten us out. We spurn such accountability at our own risk.

We need to be accountable to the Lord and others.

Day 131

Benjamin Harrison

Romans 5:3-4 "And not only that, but we also rejoice in our afflictions, because we know that affliction produces endurance, endurance produces proven character, and proven character produces hope."

Have you ever been fired? The feelings of rejection and embarrassment can be pretty brutal. Imagine what it's like basically to be fired in front of the nation by the nation. That's what Benjamin Harrison experienced in early November 1892, when he went up for re-election and didn't get it.

As tough as this was, though, it wasn't even the worst thing he was going through at that point. On October 25, 1892, Caroline Harrison, the wife of Benjamin, succumbed to tuberculosis. Put those two things together, and it was a crushing period in his life.

Hopefully, you will never experience that level of suffering.

Unfortunately for Harrison, he couldn't even go off and grieve in privacy because he wouldn't leave office until the next March. He couldn't just stop being President of the United States. The country—which had just rejected him—still needed him to do his job.

There was much work left to be done, and there was no way around it—Harrison just had to keep working.

Our burdens get heavy. At times they may seem overwhelming. And yet, if God has left us here—if we are still breathing—God's calling on our lives has not expired. Our roles change, but our calling to serve the Lord is still in effect. There is still purpose and value in our lives. Perhaps today we need to pray for the strength to just keep going.

Day 132

Ulysses Grant

Joshua 10:25A "Joshua said to them, 'Do not be afraid or discouraged, be strong and courageous.'"

On October 28, 1873, the country was experiencing one of its periodic depressions. In Dutchess County, NY, 10,000 factory workers lost their jobs on this day. But the problems were felt country-wide.

By April 1874, Congress passed the Inflation Act, which would basically dump cash into the economy to the tune of $44 million. This money would not be backed by gold, but it would make cash easier to come by.

Both parties wanted this, and Ulysses Grant was prepared to sign the legislation. But the more he studied the bill, the more he realized it went against his vision for what the federal government should do. Grant believed the government had a responsibility to keep money reliable. Flooding the market with cash would be popular in the short term, but it might not fix the economy, and it could have led to problems later. Grant vetoed the bill, despite its popularity.

Would we be brave enough to do something like that? Are we willing to go against what is popular? We usually frame the question in terms of standing up for a Christian principle in the face of sin. But what if it's your church or preacher who is doing something you believe contradicts Scripture? What if you are a preacher, and there is a practice that is popular among your congregation, but it isn't biblical?

Is today the day we need to pray for a spirit of bravery so we can stand against something that is popular but wrong?

Day 133

Herbert Hoover

Psalm 30:5 "For His anger lasts only a moment, but His favor, a lifetime. Weeping may stay overnight, but there is joy in the morning."

In the 1920s, the economy was surging. A proof of this vitality was an unemployment rate that hovered around 3-4%. One of the major factors in this was the explosive growth in new industries like cars and telephones. Thus, it was hardly shocking when Herbert Hoover said at his inauguration, "I have no fears for the future of our country."

On October 24, 1929, the Stock Market saw a huge drop in values across the board. When it took another dramatic tumble five days later on October 29, it was clear that the economy was in trouble. Unemployment would reach a staggering 23%.

Underemployment was another issue that overwhelmed Hoover. Underemployment can mean that someone is working part-time when they need to be working full-time, or the term can be applied when people are working below their talent/educational level, like if an accountant was selling apples on a street corner.

And so it goes. Sometimes life is going great, then we are blindsided. But oftentimes things turn around again. The Great Depression that started in 1929 eventually ended. Hard times don't last forever for those who are in Christ. Today, as we struggle with whatever it is we are struggling with, we just need to keep in mind that our troubles won't last. We are promised a happy ending. It might come in this life, and it might not, but we will definitely see a glorious day when Christ comes for us, or we go to Him. Let us find our peace in that truth today.

Day 134

Grover Cleveland

2 Corinthians 7:1 "So then, dear friends, since we have these promises, let us cleanse ourselves from every impurity of the flesh and spirit, bringing holiness to completion in the fear of God."

When Grover Cleveland was trying to win the presidency in 1884, his Democratic Party campaigned on the idea that he was the morally superior candidate. His opponent, Republican James Blaine from Maine, had somehow survived politically even though he had been caught taking bribes earlier in his career.

Imagine the surprise of voters, then, when it came out that Cleveland had an illegitimate child. An interview with the child's mother was published in a New York newspaper on October 31, 1884. According to the mother, the situation was not a love affair with an unintended consequence; she said that Cleveland had taken unfair advantage of her, then he and/or his friends had her sent off to an asylum, and they took her baby away.

For his part, Cleveland said the child was his, but he took no ownership of any of the rest of it. Some friends tried to suggest that the child was not his, but he was trying to protect a married friend's reputation. Cleveland was single at the time.

He won the election, but he had certainly not retained the moral high ground.

The moral of the story: Hypocrisy is an ugly look. How many famous Christians have had their reputations and their witness destroyed by moral indiscretions? But this isn't about famous Christians, or presidents, as much as it is about us. We need to strive for holiness, because when we indulge in sinful behavior, it not only takes our focus off God, but it also undermines our witness. We need to strive for holiness today.

Day 135

James Polk

1 Corinthians 10:13 "No temptation has come upon you except what is common to humanity. But God is faithful; He will not allow you to be tempted beyond what you are able, but with the temptation He will also provide a way out so that you may be able to bear it."

On November 5, 1844, Democrat James K. Polk defeated his Whig opponent Henry Clay and became the eleventh President of the United States. One of the challenges that comes with being president is dealing with people who want to gain undue influence. For example, a man tried to give Polk a fancy carriage and a horse to pull it. Later on, a group of men offered the eleventh president the same thing. In both situations, the president declined the gifts, saying they were too extravagant. Polk was suspicious of the motives of the gift givers, so he kept his guard up.

We need to be vigilant when temptation hits the second time. Some people who get into trouble with sin (adultery, porn, gossip, lack of forgiveness, whatever) actually resist it at first, then succumb later. Maybe we get cocky and let our guard down; maybe we say we tried saying no, but when the temptation hits us again, we say "I'm only human," as if that is an adequate excuse.

We all need a little James K. Polk in us. We need to keep saying no to that recurring temptation today.

Day 136

Richard Nixon

Matthew 5:44 "But I tell you, love your enemies and pray for those who persecute you."

On November 9, 1918, Spiro Agnew was born. He would grow up to become the VP under Richard Nixon. Back in the 1970s, when Nixon was the chief executive, a couple of men wrote a book about Nixon and said he wanted to suspend the Constitution and appoint Spiro Agnew to succeed him.

It was interesting that such a theory got published. As a historian, I am hesitant to look back on past events and second guess people who made wrong choices or guesses. Hindsight is 20/20, as they say. Despite my reticence, though, this idea was just…ridiculous. How in the world would Congress, the press, the military, or the American people just stand by and let Nixon destroy our democratic system? And why would he have wanted to do it for Agnew—a guy Nixon did not know well at the start of their partnership and with whom he never became close? The scenario would have been at least slightly more plausible if the writers had accused Nixon of suspending elections so he could hold onto the White House himself.

But these authors believed their theory, or at least they were convinced their readers would believe it. It is human nature to trust negative stories about people we don't like, even without proof. We need to resist that urge. The temptation to believe negative rumors and speculations about people we don't like is strong, but our God is stronger. And imagine what a powerful witness it would be if you stood up for an enemy behind the enemy's back. It could be a life-changing kind of witness. Let's pray to be that kind of witness today.

Day 137

Millard Fillmore

James 4:14B "For you are like vapor that appears for a little while, then vanishes."

November 10, 1808 was the birthdate of Lewis Charles Levin. Who is Levin? He was the founder of the Know-Nothing Party, which later became the American Party. It was an anti-immigrant party.

Why is this relevant to a book called *Devotions with Presidents*?

I'm glad I asked.

Milliard Fillmore finished out Zachary Taylor's term, but his party (the Whigs) did not want him in 1852. After he struck out with them, he became the American Party candidate in the 1856 election. He received less than twenty-five percent of the popular vote, and he only won one state.

His own party, the people who knew him best and liked him more than other people did, did not think he was a good presidential candidate. Did he really think going with a minor party was going to end in victory?

Sometimes we need to accept that certain windows of opportunity are closed. I have written elsewhere in this book that as long as we are breathing, we are supposed to serve God. But we will not always serve Him the same way. We talk in church circles about interim pastors, who are just filling in until the "permanent" pastor arrives. Really, we are all interim at whatever it is we are doing. It is a blessing to be able to accept that. Things change. Eventually, all of our work here will be done, and we will go to be with the Lord. Accepting that truth should inspire us to make the most of the time we have, and it should help us to embrace the reality that seasons change. This is God's plan for us.

Day 138

Rutherford Hayes

Luke 7:34 "The Son of Man has come eating and drinking, and you say, 'Look, a glutton and a drunkard, a friend of tax collectors and sinners.'"

Here was my plan: I would do a devotional entry on how Franklin Roosevelt supported African Americans and women by watching an African American woman sing on an Easter Sunday while he was president. This kind of spotlight and opportunity was a worthwhile effort to treat an oppressed person with dignity and send to the nation a message that pushed against bigotry.

Here's where things get interesting: Just a little research revealed that a much earlier president had already done this. It just wasn't on Easter Sunday.

On November 13, 1878, Marie Williams became the first African American singer to perform at the White House. Rutherford Hayes made this happen shortly after the end of slavery, so it was at least a little controversial. More than 1800 years earlier, Jesus consorted with tax collectors who weren't just ordinary tax men— they were Jewish men bleeding money out of their people to give it to their Roman occupiers.

Who are the unpopular ones within our own areas of influence? Who are those people in our lives who society looks down on? What can we do to communicate that they are worthy of our respect, and more importantly, God's love? Let's pray today that God would open our eyes to see such people and such opportunities.

Day 139

Rutherford Hayes

Romans 10:13-15 "For everyone who calls on the name of the Lord will be saved. How, then, can they call on Him they have not believed in? And how can they believe without hearing about Him? And how can they hear without a preacher? And how can they preach unless they are sent? As it is written: How beautiful are the feet of those who bring good news."

On November 16, 1877, Rutherford B. Hayes was president as the first telephone was installed in the White House. This was a great leap forward for technology and communication, and it would have a considerable impact on politics in Washington and the social life of the city. Important planning could happen and decisions could be made and communicated much more quickly than ever before.

Imagine, though, what people would have thought if Hayes had never used the phone—if he had never made or received calls. What difference does it make if we have the opportunity to communicate, but we choose not to?

In our situation, we have the opportunity to deliver a life-saving message of hope, but what difference does the message make if we won't deliver it? Sharing our faith can be embarrassing and difficult. One time I did such a poor job with a conversation about faith that the guy I was talking to didn't understand what I was asking him, and when we were done talking, I still couldn't tell if he was a Christian or not. But, sometimes we have to fail at something before we can figure out how to do it better.

We have the most important message in the universe. Let's pray that we would have a willingness to share it.

Day 140

Chester Arthur

Ephesians 4:29 "No foul language should come from your mouth, but only what is good for building up someone in need, so that it gives grace to those who hear."

On November 18, 1886, Chester Arthur passed away. It is as good a date as any to look at his life. He served honorably as president after owing his career to his participation in a political machine. He was part of a corrupt system, but he surprised many people by serving honorably.

Part of the problem people had with him, though, was not just his origin story; it was how he handled his election as VP.

He stood up at a celebration dinner and basically taunted the press. He went on and on about how he couldn't go into the (fishy) details of the election process because the media was there, and they might ask questions. "If it were not for the reporters, I would tell you the truth."

Perhaps Arthur was just so surprised by his success that he got a little giddy about it. Whatever the explanation, it is not a justifiable excuse for his lack of graciousness.

We need to not be jerks when things go our way. Being classy and gracious in victory is about as important as it is to be classy and gracious in defeat. Maybe we will never know the excitement of being elected vice-president, but there is still that impulse in some of us to gloat a little bit when we are proven right about something. The desire to say, "I told you so," is almost irresistible for some people. An abrasive personality can hurt us in a lot of ways. In the context of this book, it's worth noting that it can definitely hurt our witness.

Day 141

John Kennedy

Colossians 3:5-6 "Therefore, put to death what belongs to your earthly nature: sexual immorality, impurity, lust, evil desire, and greed, which is idolatry. Because of these, God's wrath is coming upon the disobedient."

On November 22, 1963, John Kennedy was assassinated, and the last rites were performed over him, as is customary for Catholics. It would be the kind of thing that one might guess would happen, given that it is well known that Kennedy was Catholic.

Interestingly, though, this was the fourth time the last rites were performed over Kennedy. He beat the odds several times, but he couldn't beat them forever.

Neither can we.

Maybe we are taking risks we shouldn't be taking. Kennedy was certainly a risk-taker. He served in the US Navy during World War Two, which wasn't the safest career choice. But at least in that case he was defending America and fighting for democracy. He was also a risk-taker when it came to his serial womanizing. He had such a problem here that his wife almost left him, which would have been a career-killer for a politician in the 1950s and 1960s.

Today's devotion, of course, is not really about Kennedy; it's about us. What risky behavior are we indulging in? Are we flirting, stealing from our employer, or cheating on our taxes? Do we have a secret addiction to alcohol, painkillers, or porn? We need to stop. If we can't stop on our own, we need to pray about it and get whatever counseling or help we need on top of that. We need to cut out the risky behavior, because the consequences are hurting us even before we get caught.

Day 142

Abraham Lincoln

Ephesians 6:14 "Stand, therefore, with truth like a belt around your waist, righteousness like armor on your chest."

December 6, 1847, is the date when Abraham Lincoln was sworn in for his one and only term in the House of Representatives. Surprisingly, there is no greater meaning in Lincoln only serving a single term there. He had pledged to do no more than that because it was a tradition in his district. The idea was that constantly rotating young men in and out of that seat would give a lot of men an exciting opportunity to serve their district and raise their visibility and career prospects.

What makes this so interesting is people over the years have created a narrative about Lincoln's incredible perseverance despite an extraordinary number of setbacks. It's an inspirational tale of grit. His "failure" to get reelected to the House is part of the narrative, but it's false. There is no great story of grit to be learned from this particular event. Sure, Lincoln had some experience with failure—almost everyone does—but his story was not that of a guy with an unusually long string of bad luck who persevered anyway and ended up with the biggest job in the country.

We need to be careful of this as Christians. Sometimes we latch onto an inspirational tale or a story that fits our preferred political narrative, and we want to use it even when the evidence is there to prove that it is false. We think the accuracy of the story doesn't matter because we like the way it makes us feel. We have to be careful because there are people who don't want to believe that Jesus is the Truth. We can't give nonbelievers ammunition and excuses to not believe. Let us pray today to be speakers of the Truth, even when that gets in the way of a good story.

Day 143

Franklin Pierce

Psalm 32:8 "I will instruct you and show you the way to go; with my eye on you, I will give counsel."

On December 7, 1838, Anna Kendrick Pierce died. She was an alcoholic. Her son, Franklin Pierce was good looking, charming, and a war hero. But he was also an alcoholic.

Did he share this trait with his mother because of nature or nurture? Was he genetically predisposed to drink to excess, or did he handle life's stresses in the same way that his mother modeled for him? Was it a combination of both?

Whatever the reasons behind it, Franklin Pierce drank too much, and it would have been better for him to just put the bottle down.

Of course, that's easy for me to say—I don't drink, so alcohol has never had a hold on me. But there are a lot of addictions out there that one might struggle with. Those of us who get in front of other people and talk, or make music, or act, might easily become addicted to the adulation of strangers.

I once heard that "serious gamers" average twenty hours a week on their craft, which, unless one is getting paid, seems like poor stewardship of time. (I realize that was the most overtly judgmental thing I have ever written on a behavior that the Bible is silent about, but, come on, twenty hours a week of gaming sounds like *a lot*.)

My point is not to minimize the sin of drunkenness; it is to say that many of us struggle with temptations. Sometimes the sins of the mother (in the case of Mrs. Pierce) or the father can impact our children, or our spouses, or our parents. Let us today pray for guidance to get the help we need so we can be who we need to be for those who depend on us.

Day 144

Thomas Jefferson

Romans 10:1 "Brothers and sisters, my heart's desire and prayer to God concerning them is for their salvation."

On December 8, 1784, Jefferson wrote to Madison about Patrick Henry. "What we have to do, I think, is devoutly to pray for his death."

Jefferson was kidding, of course.

He didn't *devoutly* pray about anything.

But the issue for us today is what we are doing when it comes to prayer. Do we lack the patience/faith/character to pray devoutly? Are we praying for things that aren't good? Maybe we aren't praying for the death of our political enemies (or maybe some of us are!), but perhaps our prayers are a different kind of selfish. Are we neglecting to pray for the spiritually lost and/or hurting who are around us?

In a lot of churches, prayer times have become reduced to hospital reports and health-related requests. There is nothing wrong with that, except perhaps when we spend more time praying for sick Christians than we do for people who are spiritually lost. Where is the sense of urgency? Where are the prayers for those people in our lives who are not around other Christians—those who are only around us? Are we afraid if we ask God to reach out to a lost person, He will ask us to do the same?

Praying for the sick is a theologically sound thing to do; there is nothing wrong with it, but some of us need to get serious about praying for nonbelievers. Let's do that today.

Day 145

James Buchanan

1 Corinthians 16:14 "Do everything in love."

December 9, 1819, was a tragic day for the family of Anne Caroline Coleman. She died young and suddenly. Shortly before this, she had broken off her engagement with James Buchanan, the future fifteenth President of the United States.

Buchanan was told he wasn't welcome at the funeral. I include that information just because it's weird and interesting, but we don't know the reason for it, so let's move on.

Buchanan never pursued another woman. Did he love Anne that much? Maybe. Some speculated that he just wasn't interested in women, and after Anne, he didn't bother to pretend that he was.

The Bible says it is not good for man to be alone. The context of that passage is marriage, but the principle extends beyond that. After all, Jesus never married (unless you want to argue that His bride is the Church).

We need to not be an island. We need to be relational. How can we fulfill God's commands to love one another, our neighbors, or our enemies, if we are isolating ourselves?

We need relationships. We need to be loving other people today. For some of us, that's a stretch, but stretching isn't a bad thing. Let's pray today that the Lord would help us to love a little more than we feel like loving.

Day 146

Abraham Lincoln

Psalm 34:14 "Turn away from evil and do what is good; seek peace and pursue it."

December 13, 1818, was the birthdate of Mary Todd Lincoln. She had four brothers who fought for the Confederacy, and she tended to rub people the wrong way, as I mentioned earlier in this book. People didn't like her, and that would not be such a big deal were it not for the consequences of that dislike.

It is an interesting aspect of human nature that when people do not like someone, they tend to believe the worst about that person. Thus, when people started gossiping that Mrs. Lincoln was a Confederate spy, a lot of people thought it might be true, even though there was no real evidence to support such a belief.

The thing is, the rumor did not just hurt the reputation of Mary Todd Lincoln; it also had an impact on her husband. Abraham Lincoln was forced to address Congress and declare that his wife was not a spy for the South.

He didn't need that. The Civil War was the most divisive event in American history. Because, understandably, people cared about it so much, they had passionate opinions on how we should be conducting the war. Success was not coming as fast as people in the North thought it should. Many blamed Lincoln. As thousands kept dying each month, many blamed Lincoln. He had a lot going on, and the last thing he needed was to have to fight a public relations battle on behalf of his wife, who had turned rubbing people the wrong way into an art form.

We should think about how our personalities and interactions impact our loved ones, and how they impact our witness. Maybe some of us need to pray for a good disposition today.

Day 147

William Howard Taft

Luke 6:36 "Be merciful, just as your Father also is merciful."

The United States claimed control of the Philippines on December 21, 1898. The Philippines had been a colony of Spain, but with the onset of the Spanish-American War, the US decided to hit Spain where it was vulnerable.

By the year 1900, the US was firmly in control and President William McKinley handed William Howard Taft the responsibility of establishing a civilian-run government over the islands instead of a military one. The previous governor had been pretty heavy-handed, but Taft was sympathetic to the native people and benevolent in his treatment of them.

This was especially impressive back then, given how rampant racism was toward indigenous peoples. And the Filipino people were not the most compliant. Understandably, they resented trading in one group of domineering and exploitative outsiders for another. Thus, if Taft had decided to rule with an iron fist, it would have been unsurprising. But he chose benevolence.

Do we possess the gift of mercy? Are we thoughtful and patient when we have power over others? For those of us who are bosses and/or parents, do the people under our authority know what mercy looks like because they have seen it in us?

We need God's mercy to save our souls. Let us today pray that we can model that kind of mercy for someone else.

Day 148

James Monroe

John 15:13 "No one has greater love than this: to lay down his life for his friends."

Millions of Americans spend December 25 each year celebrating the birth of Christ and opening gifts—not necessarily in that order, but that's a devotion for another day. December 26 is spent returning a significant percentage of those gifts in exchange for something else. Oh, and let's not forget the redeeming of gift cards.

For James Monroe, who would later become our fifth president, December 26 held a different significance: It was on that day in 1776 when he was shot in the shoulder at the Battle of Trenton during the Revolutionary War. He believed in the cause of freedom, and he was willing to pay the price.

We believe in the cause of Christ, but what price are we willing to pay? Increasingly, many Christians have trouble just showing up at church four times a month and worshipping God with other believers. And what do we do with our money? Too many of us say giving ten percent is just Old Testament law, and I think a reasonable person could make a good argument for or against that, but where does that leave us? Do we recognize that we are rich compared to people in biblical times and give more than ten percent? No, most of us give way less and tell ourselves we're giving sacrificially because, really, any amount represents a sacrifice. Please note: I am not on a church staff, so it puts no money in my pocket when I challenge you to put more in the offering plate.

James Monroe risked his life for our freedom. Jesus laid down His life for our souls. Let us pray today for the faith to have a similar level of commitment.

Day 149

Franklin Pierce

Ephesians 4:31 "Let all bitterness, anger and wrath, shouting and slander be removed from you, along with all malice."

On December 30, 1853, a negotiator named James Gadsden signed the agreement that became known as the Gadsden Purchase with Mexico during Franklin Pierce's presidency.

Coming just a few years after the Mexican War, this could definitely be classified as a surprising development. It was not a shock that the United States made the offer. There was a lot of excitement in the land about a transcontinental railroad—railroad lines that could move people, goods, and mail from one side of the United States to the other. The big question was whether these side-to-side rail lines would run along the northern area of the country or the southern. Eventually, there would be multiple lines, so both bases would be covered. But in 1853, advocates of the southern route needed to find a way around the mountains out West. The land that Mr. Gadsden purchased ended up extending the southern boundaries of New Mexico and Arizona, and it made the southern route feasible.

Thus, the Americans' interest in the land was not surprising, but the willingness of Mexico to sell it to us would have been unexpected by those who knew the recent history of the two countries. The US had just won a war with Mexico in the 1840s and basically took the northern half of their country away from them.

Maybe Mexico was afraid that if they didn't agree to sell the land Gadsden wanted, we would just take it.

Still, Mexico could have fought us, but chose not to. Sometimes peace and forgiveness require a sacrifice, but what Mexico got (money and the avoidance of a great loss of life) made it worth it. Let us pray today for the peace that comes when we forgive others.

Day 150

George Washington and Thomas Jefferson

Ephesians 4:32 "And be kind and compassionate to one another, forgiving one another, just as God also forgave you in Christ."

George Washington did not have many men who answered directly to him as president, but the people he did have were quite the dream team. John Adams was VP, Alexander Hamilton was the Secretary of the Treasury, and Thomas Jefferson was the secretary of state. But as with many teams that look like a dream on paper, things were not as perfect as people thought they might be.

Thomas Jefferson in particular was very unhappy with Washington's vision for the federal government. Rather than openly criticize the president's politics, which would have reflected poorly on Jefferson, the secretary of state made disparaging personal remarks behind Washington's back. Jefferson started whispering that the old general was just not as sharp as he used to be in his younger days.

Loyalty to Washington was such that word got back to him about what was being said and by whom.

Sadly, the men couldn't reconcile, and perhaps the nation was the poorer for it. On December 31, 1793, Jefferson resigned as secretary of state.

Isn't it interesting that the two stories with the latest dates in the year both deal with forgiveness? Why, it's almost as if forgiveness is really hard, and we have to hear the same thing twice. Forgiveness is a necessity for us as believers. Is there someone in our lives we are harboring a grudge against? We should ask God for the strength to let it go.

Bonus Devotion

By Kristin Haney

2 Corinthians 1:3-4 "Blessed be the God and Father of our Lord Jesus Christ, the Father of mercies and the God of all comfort. He comforts us in all our affliction, so that we may be able to comfort those who are in any kind of affliction, through the comfort we ourselves receive from God."

Probably for obvious reasons, Christmas has been my favorite among the Christian holidays since I was a child. I still thoroughly enjoy it, but my holiday favoritism has shifted as an adult who wrestles with more than just a pesky little brother. Adulting has recently required me to wrestle with the confusion and disappointment of unanswered prayers. Therefore, one moment of Easter has become a new favorite of mine. That moment is Easter Saturday. Yes, I meant Saturday—that wasn't a typo! When we talk about Easter, we usually think about the joy and fun of Sunday, but that's just the finale! The Easter story really comprises three days: Friday, the crucifixion day; Saturday, the waiting day; and Sunday, the resurrection day. Because we know how the story ends, none of us really sits around considering today's parallel truths from that long-ago awful day in the middle.

Reeling from the fresh pain, trauma, and stranded hope of the crucifixion is where the disciples found themselves that Saturday. Attempting to comprehend what they knew had been divinely dealt but struggling in the tension between very evident pain and only apparent promise. Of course, they hadn't experienced the restored joy and reestablished hope of Resurrection Sunday like we have. The three days of Easter sure seem applicable as an ultra-condensed picture of the Christian human life to me!

The hopes and prayers of these co-laborers of Jesus went unresolved this Saturday as they grieved. Though I imagine it was an immense comfort to bear the burden of that pain together, not even proximity to others with similar emotional wounds was enough to restore their hope. It wasn't until Jesus Himself appeared on Sunday (and the forty days after) and bared His own scars that they were once again not only full of hope, but also full of courage to the point of death. It was His return, vulnerability, and compassion that reignited their faith and action.

On that Saturday, the disciples were no doubt frustrated by unmet expectations of Jesus. Living in this world is a lot like living on a prolonged Saturday of Easter. Much like the disciples, #ChristiansOf2019 are good at making plans. While they had expectations of and plans for Jesus to conquer the Roman Empire and reign on earth in their lifetime, we have not so dissimilar plans for Jesus in our world and lives. So when Jesus willingly died instead, talk about plans gone awry!

In our modern world, when things go wrong or feel uneasy, we want it fixed quick, fast, and in a hurry. We like comfort. It's comfortable! Our emotions are beautiful and pesky. They are a gift from heaven but can also be used as a distraction from the enemy. We must take our emotions captive as we should our thoughts (2 Corinthians 10:5). I say that as one who is still making imperfect progress in that area. Here's one thing I'm learning in the middle of grappling with my own emotions and laments to God: When I choose to believe God isn't being efficient and/or sensitive enough to my pain and therefore I attempt to hastily assuage my situation with my own plans... it tends to only exhaust my resolve to hope. I believe that is where we find most people today—taking hurried action as a response to ease emotional burdens, then finding themselves too exhausted by their own fruitless efforts to even hope.

Finding ourselves sitting in the authenticity of bitter lament from the disappointment of unanswered prayers isn't a sin; it's our behavior in response that makes all the difference. Lamentations is a book literally dedicated to the grievances of human hurt, and probably the most well-known book of sorrow is Job. Unresolved prayers require a resolved faith because pain will come regardless of our attempts to stop or alleviate it (John 16:33). It is possible to navigate disappointment without losing faith. We must be ready to live from hard-earned truth gleaned by everyday experiences with

Jesus. I believe that one of the secrets of the original disciples' to maintaining faith was their relationship cultivated from years of walking with the Lord. Likewise, we can hold our spiritual ground when discomfort and pain abound through that same relationship. We were never assured comfort in this life—quite the opposite in fact. (John 16:33) What we are assured of as believers is having the Holy Spirit, the Comforter, living inside of us. Because of that, we are asked in 2 Corinthians 1:3-4 to share Him by comforting others with compassion.

On Resurrection Sunday, Jesus brought compassion via His literal open wounds as the bridge to a renewed relationship with them. Compassion is a catalyst for hope. It is the very reason we ought to offer compassion freely to others. What if we were people who vulnerably shared the scars of our lives through intentional relationships like Jesus did with the disciples? What if we treated our painful wounds not as a disgrace, but instead like the marks of the Lion of Judah they were meant to be? Scars are evidence that you survived. My dad told me once, "If you're a Christian, scars are God's mark on your life, and we should wear them proudly." Not proud in the sense of arrogance, but proud because we can boast that we survived not by our strength, but His (2 Cor. 12:9). The product of that kind of compassion begun on Resurrection Sunday and christened at Pentecost is still changing the world.

We are the descendants of that miraculous Sunday, filled with the comfort of the Holy Spirit so that we can give it at will to others who desperately need the hope of heaven! It's a quiet danger to the Enemy to stand firm with the conviction of knowing God as Ebenezer (He has) and Jehovah-Jireh (He will) in our life. That kind of counter-culture faith looks like compassion regardless of personal comfort. Jesus demonstrated that compassion can prayerfully give birth to a saving faith for the unsaved and a restored faith for the shipwrecked Christian. *That* is the power of Resurrection Sunday we want when we are stuck besieged by the same emotions that afflicted the disciples on that less acclaimed Holy Saturday.

I would argue that our perception of silence from heaven is mistaken when it comes to unanswered prayers because we are deaf and blind to what God is maneuvering in the spiritual realm on our behalf. We are never asked to take charge of these invisible heavenly battles; rather we are asked to put on our armor, go to the battle, and stand firm to bear witness to the already won victory (Ephesians 6:11, 2 Chronicles 20). We take our positions looking out from victory, not for it. So when we come to God with our pain, let us honestly temper our prayers for His kingdom to come and will to be done on earth as it is in heaven, by also admitting (not just to our sympathetic friends) that we sometimes lament living in a reality that requires we occasionally yield to the mystery of unanswered prayer. He is compassionate to your misery. If His will is not to rescue us from "it," we can rest assured He is faithful to sustain us through "it." Sunday *is* coming. I'll leave you to ponder what I have been "what-iffing" recently, only please do so with your name inserted: What-if the (admittedly less dramatic, but nevertheless raw) circumstances surrounding my unanswered prayer all began with a familiar OT heavenly conversation that went something like, "Have you considered my servant Kristin" (Job 2:3)?

Challenge: Read the book of Job. Elihu was the only friend that correctly discerned Job's problem. Pray that you can be the Elihu in the stories of others; the friend who with divinely cultivated discernment and convictional compassion speaks into the lives of others and tells them of the only everlasting hope that comes from Jesus.

About the Author

Timothy D. Holder is a professor of History at Walters State Community College where he is also an assistant dean, and he rather frequently serves as a guest preacher in various churches. With a Ph. D. and Masters in History, and a Masters in Applied Theology to go along with a BA in Bible, Holder's two lifelong fields of study, his two passions, come together in *Devotions with Presidents*. He lives in Knoxville, Tennessee.

If you enjoyed *Devotions with Presidents*, please consider writing a review at Amazon.com or GoodReads.com.

Other Books by the Author

Presidential Stories: A Different Kind of Devotional

Presidential Character: George Washington through John Quincy Adams

Presidential Trivia 2.0